SELLING
LIKE A SOLDIER

MASTER THE SELLING PROCESS

with
salesguru

NITIN KHURANA

www.whitefalconpublishing.com

Selling Like A Soldier
Nitin Khurana

www.whitefalconpublishing.com

All rights reserved
First Edition, 2023
© Nitin Khurana, 2023
Cover design by White Falcon Publishing, 2023
Cover image source freepik.com

No part of this publication may be reproduced, or stored in a retrieval system, or transmitted in any form by means of electronic, mechanical, photocopying or otherwise, without prior written permission from the author.

The contents of this book have been certified and timestamped on the Gnosis blockchain as a permanent proof of existence. Scan the QR code or visit the URL given below to verify the blockchain certification for this book.

Scan To View Blockchain Certification

The views expressed in this work are solely those of the author and do not reflect the views of the publisher, and the publisher hereby disclaims any responsibility for them.

Requests for permission should be addressed to
nitinkhurana@hotmail.com

ISBN - 978-1-63640-780-7

Message from the author

I would like to dedicate this book to all the "sales-gurus" I have met, who helped me understand and internalise that "selling is a process and we need to follow it religiously".

In this book, I have explained various stages of selling processes. I have compared a salesperson to a soldier for various reasons.

This book is a reference book for young entrepreneurs/ start-ups who sometimes get lost while handling their routine work. This book will also help middle management of corporate companies who are working in sales function to revisit their selling process and be the "salesguru" for junior management and management trainees working with them.

Sales leaders who build strong foundations by creating and periodically reviewing sales process are always appreciated as trendsetter paving way in the right direction.

Finally I would like to thank my family and friends who constantly motivated me to write this book.

Special thanks my friend Mr. Gaurav Mohunta, a renowned advocate for taking out time and capering proof reading of this book. Lastly thanks to my daughter Rahini Khurana and my wife Neha Khurana for their encouragement and cooperation.

With best wishes,
NITIN KHURANA

Contents

Part I Practices

1. Salesperson is like a Soldier 3
2. Excuse can't Rescue 8
3. Accept Criticism 14
4. Challenge Yourself 20

Part II Productivity

5. Be Self Disciplined 27
6. Goal Setting 34
7. Time Management 41
8. Sales Mindset 48

Part III Preparation

9. Become the Product Expert 55
10. Customer Segmentation 61
11. Market Penetration 68

12. The Sales Pitch 73

Part IV Prospecting

13. Marketing Tools 83
14. Lead Generation 89
15. Sales Funnel: Creating & Managing IDEA 96

Part V Perform

16. Quotes and Follow Up 103
17. Telling isn't Selling 107
18. Handle Objections 115
19. Sales Negotiation 118

Part VI Post-Sales

20. Customer Support and Service 125
21. Relationship Management 131
22. Customer Feedback & Evaluation 134

Part I

Practices

Chapter 1

Salesperson is like a Soldier

A salesperson can be often mistaken for not working smartly, as their work is only measured by the outcome. Everyone around only care about results i.e. sales number. Focus on Sales is a very natural phenomenon, as Sales number define the top line of any business. Hence in this rush for numbers, salesperson/ team tends to ignore the sales process.

When the sales process is not followed among the members of the sales team, then the outcome i.e. sales numbers are bound to decline. Therefore an organisation must cultivate the habit of following the sales process among their salesperson and sales team.

A salesperson is a self-motivated person. He or She is naturally enthusiastic and passionate about selling. They don't need external motivation all the time. If their passion is triggered then they will go all out for it with full enthusiasm. It's similar to that of a soldier. If a soldier hates the enemy then he will be naturally self-motivated to run up the hill. He does it without even thinking.

Similarly, if a salesperson is motivated then he will find means to reach the client and build up a good database of the prospective customer in his respective region. A good salesperson will always look for customers and make sales happen. A good salesperson will be process-oriented which will drive him for results. Hence a good salesperson will achieve his sales target.

Therefore, good soldiering and top-selling are comparable.

Let's begin with what makes a good soldier. Although it is difficult to completely define a patriot, here are few items worth considering for comparison to a salesperson:

Both are on their respective **frontlines**. For a Soldier, the border is front line whereas for a Salesperson they being the interface between customers and company, they become the face of the company. A Soldier might actually die while fighting for their country but the salespersons will not have to lay down their lives except to just hold out their hearts.

Training is part of their routine. A periodical and regular training are structured into their objective. Soldier gets trained indoor and outdoor, in the field with mock drills and warrior tasks. A top salesperson makes training and coach part of his annual plan and budget.

If a soldier who isn't trained for going into the battlefield will stay safe in his office only because he won't be prepared. However, a salesperson who isn't trained in selling, products and services understanding and people skills will not be safe in their office as well. He will be labelled as non-performer and sooner or later, he can be replaced.

Equip: A soldier is responsible for the ownership and maintaining the weapons clothed to them. A salesperson becomes top salesperson when he equips himself with ABC (attitude, belief system and character) skills through reading, training and learnings from lost sales. These skills set will make selling smooth and faster for the salesperson.

Thus, A salesperson's ABC (attitude, belief system and character) needs to be equipped to maintain and upgrade as needed.

Admirable: Being a soldier is one of the most admirable profession. This profession is described with words like courage and loyalty.

As far as selling goes, many of our own personal buying experiences are negative. Most of the people believe that the process of selling is manipulative, aggressive, shady and so on.

Soldier takes pride in their profession is often driven by the admirable words they hear. We as salespersons should also focus on selling experience where customers raved about us. We must think of the time when our customer admired us for honesty, dependability, quality product and services. When we worked and went an extra mile just to see pride and delight on the face of our customer.

We have to believe those words like a soldier.

Fighting for a cause. A Soldier is always ready for a fight and to get deployed as they believe in the purpose of their fight. They never question the order.

Similarly, a salesperson must have a strong belief in their products and themselves as a service provider. Self-doubts, low confidence, procrastination or giving up perseverance can keep us believing in the market slump, which will keep us away from the very people who want our services.

A salesperson must always be willing to fight to help their customer.

Services before self: "Something greater than themselves" is the belief soldiers carry on the front lines. Similarly for the salesperson putting "Product/ services before self" will reflect on

Salesperson is like a Soldier

the true value of what that product/service does for the end-user.

Keeping the value, the benefit, of what our product and service can do for our customer above ourself will give us the strength to overcome procrastination on the prospecting process i.e cold calling or follow up.

Challenges: Every task for a soldier is a different task, which a soldier needs to accept as a challenge. It becomes the need of the hour similarly, for the salesperson, every task is an independent challenge, where they need to prove themselves.

Thus just like different challenging situations makes a soldier mentally tough; similarly such situations too makes salespersons mentally tough.

Selling can be an individual's success. However, an organisation wins when all the sales team are selling. Therefore, Winning belongs to everyone. When a soldier wins, it isn't his personal victory but the victory to the entire army and the nation. Hence, it is very important for salespersons to understand that if they win; then it becomes a victory for everyone.

There are NO winners in a losing team.

Similarly, a salesperson must never take losing orders/ contracts or customers personally.

Hence it will not be wrong to compare the likes of a soldier to that of a salesperson. Therefore, it is for us as sales professionals to think and introspect about "what kind of examples we set for next-generation salesperson and the society".

If we want results of good selling to be like that of good soldiers, then actions are important. Definitely, there is no absolute, or concrete quality of good soldiering. However, there are good

Practices

soldiers and top salespeople.

Everyone loves winning, but not everyone can actually win like a soldier. To be treated like a soldier, a salesperson must act like one.

Chapter 2

Excuse can't Rescue

"Loser makes excuse, Winner brings an end to the excuse"

In sales, the salesperson who uses excuse to justify poor performance rather than proactively work on it and find new methods to perform, often remains at the bottom of the success ladder.

Some of the excuses which we often hear from salesperson are listed below:

1. The market is drying up
2. Our prices are high
3. Leads are weak
4. Customer is not ready yet
5. The target is unrealistic
6. Our Product/ services aren't good enough
7. I forgot to follow up
8. I couldn't get hold of him
9. I didn't know that I should chase him

Practices

10. Seniors don't support

11. My territory is smaller than others

12. My pipeline is stacked for next month

13. They're happy with their current supplier

14. GDP is not growing

15. They aren't in office to make decision

16. No one is getting back to me

17. No one knows who we are

18. Our competitor is the best

19. I've been busy doing other things

20. We are too expensive

21. Marketing has no impact

22. It's not my job

23. Marketing material is outdated

24. Competitor prices are very low

25. We don't advertise

26. Our visibility is low

27. Rejections wipe me out

28. I don't like making cold calls

29. Their BOD will take the final call

30. They used our proposal to get better prices

31. Businesses aren't spending

32. Government policy isn't clear

33. Their consultant is not recommending us

This list can be endless. Being a salesperson we need to introspect "Is that all we can do?".

Here are the main excuses salespeople make to run away from taking responsibility:

- Company pricing,
- Competition,
- The economy,
- Lack of efforts.

These factors are External factors i.e. Company pricing, competition and the economy are not in the salesperson's control, therefore salespersons cant control. Hence let us focus on the internal factors i.e. *lack of efforts.*

Responsibility is the degree which a salesperson accepts for showing up results rather than justifying or making excuses.

Irrespective of conditions surrounding them, a salesperson who has a strong sense of responsibility will find a way to get the necessary amount of sales. They'll do so by controlling the one factor which is controllable, and i.e. they themselves!

Practices

Unfortunately, 60% of salespeople don't take responsibility for their results.

There will always be unfavourable uncontrollable elements which will influence their numbers like a weakening economy, products issues, and sometimes competitors who throw away their product. In these situations, when most salespeople tend to throw down their arms and give up, a few topline salesperson still manage to be successful. 10% to be precise.

This 10% will do everything they can to stay in control of their productivity.

How do they do it? They stay focused on their activities. They keep their productivity. They also make sure to be consultative and pay attention to the needs of their clients.

No matter the length of a salesperson's career, they will most likely go through economic upturns and downfalls. In fact, the longer their career, the more they'll experience the cycle.

Their level of responsibility depends on how they react. If they're reactive by responding to uncontrollable elements, rather than the controllable ones, they'll fall prey to the circumstances.

Don't let uncontrollable elements affect their attitude. If they let this happen, they'll experience a loss of morale, which will affect their will to sell.

The sales process and responsibility

When a salesperson is low on morale, they might lose the motivation to make cold calls, would become less committed and complacent, not only to their success but to the needs of their clients.

However, the idea here is to be aware of the situations which can affect their success and in turn the company's topline. In fact, the salesperson must acknowledge the situation if they're to have a clear grasp of their circumstances. However, they must consciously decide not to let themselves deviate from their objectives.

Bring down their barriers

The outside factors attracting salespersons to give up are just excuses stopping them from getting where they need to go. Ultimately, taking responsibility for their actions and say to themselves, "I'm the only person standing in my way of what I want to achieve."

"If you should change one thing tomorrow when you get into the office, it should be to stop excuse making! If salespeople say they can't get the business because of X and Y reasons, they're not taking responsibility for their actions." —Dave Kurlan, Two Minutes on Excuse Making

The minute a salesperson admits to not getting business due to their own fault, instead of blaming a bad economy or cheap competitive pricing, then the next question comes: "What could I have done differently?" Once a rep become aware and acknowledge their share of responsibility, they start getting different results.

Nothing can change until then.

Turning your lemons into lemonade

Every person's level of responsibility will vary. While 40% of salespeople are in the high range, this still leaves the greater majority who have very high tendencies for excuse making. The fortunate thing is that responsibility is easily fixed.

Remember

As parents we're keen on calling out lack of responsibility in our

Practices

children, though we often fail to recognize this weakness many of us have carried into our adulthood. Our natural inclination when faced with the weak performance or failure is defensiveness.

Stand up in the face of adversity and resist its influence on your fate. Every time you say, "No, this will not take me down" is an instance bringing you closer to your success.

Say it aloud "I take full responsibility" and feel the power and freedom that come with this statement. Your success will follow

We live in abudance, we have access to a lot of resources, information and knowledge data. Hence looking at possibilities is much easier these days. We must keep reviewing our processes and strategy.

Consider this research insight from the founder of Marketing Wizdom, Robert Clay: he states that

44% of salespeople give up after one negative response,

22% after two negative responses, 14% after three, and

12% after four.

Clay's cited research also shows that some 80% of prospects say no four times before agreeing to a sale– meaning over 90% of salespeople are not selling to their full potential.

Customers need keeps changing time to time, hence a salesperson should always keeps learning and updating his knowledge. Therefore a salesperson must have that inbuilt flexibility and habit to keep learning.

Chapter 3

Accept Criticism

"Criticism like appreciation is also a feedback. Therefore when we accept appreciation with pleasure, we must accept criticism with same enthusasim."

Dealing with criticism is part of being professional.

A salesperson can anticipate outcome for their actions and evaluate alternatives before implementing them. They should not react to criticism but accept suggestions and analysis from different prospectives. Being defensive to criticism puts us on back foot thus reducing the chances of improvement.

"No one who can't delight in the discovery of his own mistakes deserves to be called a scholar". We have rarely seen people coming forward and accepting their mistakes voluntarily. No one likes to listen that they're wrong or that they're not working to their potential. When you are working, it is natural that you might make some mistakes, but not accepting those might make you rework again and again and thus can lead to deteriotiation of your work performance and your reputation. On other hand, accepting feedback will enable you to improve your proformance.

However some people can accept criticism, whether it's positive or negative, whereas others don't know how to deal with it. Dealing with critisim is a skill and it can be learnt.

It's an essential business skill.

A natural reaction to critiscism is being defensive. Instead of defending yourself or getting angry, when someone brings you a piece of constructive criticism it is better to take their feedback without reacting. Any kind of negative reaction to such situation will make you look bad and you might be refered as someone who cant handle criticism.

Furthermore, anger stops you from thinking and learning. The moment you get angry because a colleague or senior says you are wrong or need to improve in a particular area, that's the time you've lost the plot.

Someone with first instinct to get angry or justify their actions cant learn and grow.

Relax, Take a breath and watch it out.

Ask yourself,

1. Why am I so defensive?
2. Why do I feel this way rather than simply dealing with positive and negative criticism?

Mostly people react or get angry to suggestions or positive critiscm because of ego and pride. It becomes embarrassing for some. It can make them feel insignicifant and ashamed. They might have trouble in admitting that they are wrong or there's something deeper in your mind.

A defensive attitude is hurdle in career/ business growth, making it worth your time to discover why your ego makes dealing with criticism so difficult.

If you find it difficult to handle, then it is worth exploring.

Accept Criticism

Mistakes aren't failures

Mistakes shouldn't be labelled as failures. There is always scope of improvement in whatever we do. Need of improvement doesn't mean failure. Considering mistakes as failure is one of the main reason we might act defensively while reacting to critical feedback.

Concluding that you are bad at your job, just because you need improvement is unjustified and unfair. However these feedbacks should become your lessons. You need to know these in order to make self improvement. Learning is a continuous process and we learn while we work. No one goes into a job knowing all the details or knowing everything correctly. Provide yourself tools, time and space to learn and grow. Learning and adopting is the way forward.

Positive critiscm enables improvement

You would be expected to consider positive and negative critism. After considering the kind of critism and its origin, you can accept it. If you accept it, then go till the bottom and ensure it isn't repeated again. To get better, work on constructive feedback.

If you're a sales manager, you may stagnate in your job without you opening yourself up to the opinions and advice of your superiors and colleagues. You actually tend to demonstrate your strength if you accept criticism. By doing this, you're actually taking steps to become a star salesperson. Your bosses will see that you take their criticism and apply it immediately to your work, which reflects well on you.

Consider the source

Not all criticism is constructive or even conducive. You always have to consider the source. You can't discount advice just because it comes from someone you don't like. A manager or supervisor with whom you don't get along can still offer helpful advice. Don't feel that you must accept a lecture from someone who finds mistake with everything you do or does a poor job on their own.

Your wisdom lies in your ability to differentiate between constructive and destructive criticism

You're under no compulsion to blindly accept all the criticism. You must always consider who's offering the critique and also need to think about why and where this criticism comes from; especially if it's coming from a positive or negative place. It's sad but true that people sometimes bring down others, particularly in a work environment. If a piece of critique seems spiteful, vindictive, or far-fetched, trust your instincts and ask for a second opinion. You might receive advice that's designed to bring you down rather than increase your performance, so don't hesitate to ask other managers and leaders for their opinions.

Pay attention to what's said

Many salesperson get defensive to criticism. Instead of being defensive, be mindful and pay attention to what your coworker or supervisor says. Don't allow your emotions to get in the way of the message. While dealing with criticism, once you open up to it, you normally discover easier or more efficient ways to accomplish your tasks at work. Furthermore, the advice you receive from your boss or leader can help you discover your strengths and weaknesses as an employee, but you won't learn those lessons if you refuse to let yourself listen them. It's unlikely that any manager will want to continue working with someone who shuts down their critiques.

Own what you do instead of trying to justify yourself

When faced with criticism many of salesperson starts to explain themselves. Jumping to explain yourself might makes you look

Accept Criticism

guilty, unwilling to listen and stubborn. It's upsetting and suggests that you don't possess the qualities of a valuable employee. Therefore ask yourself why your first instinct is to justify. Are there any explanations for your mistake or are you just letting your pride to speak up instead of acknowledging that you aren't perfect? Stop clarifying your mistakes and own up to them instead. You'll learn more. Further your manager/ co-worker will have more respect for you.

Review your feedback with questions

To express that you're not only listening but also dealing with the criticism in a constructive and worthwhile manner, talk to your boss about the situations. You should ask for specific instances regarding your mistakes and performance. Further ask for advice about how to appropriately perform the task. If you have issues with accomplishing a job the way your boss expects you to do it, then be honest and tell your manager how and why you're having the problems. Being truthful and taking a proactive approach will impress them.

Look for outside support

You might need outside help. That's fine, in fact needing help does not make you a failure or a weak person. It's time to move away fromthat mindset or else you'll never reach the heights of success you dreamt of. Identify your problem area and try to take help of colleagues who excel in those areas. It can be meaningful to find a work mentor who can give you tips, look over your work, and tread you in the right direction. Your bosses will take notice. Everyone love the employees who take the bull by the horns and address their issues themselves.

Practices

Ask for appraisal (follow-up on criticism)

After having understood your criticism, the professional and impressive way of dealing with criticism is to use it. The advice you receive through criticism, put it into action and then ask for a follow up review. This demonstrates to your manager that you acknowledge feedback and is taking corrective actions. This is also one of the way to build a authentic reputation in your organisation.

If the changes you make, can please your manager, improve your performance, and make you look good, then those are definetly worth it.

Don't take it personally

In a professional space, there is no room for taking criticism personally. Unless it's destructive criticism coming from a negative person or place, critique isn't personal. You are there to perform and not for being singled out by management for no reason. Your managers simply saw a inefficiency in your performance, your leadership style, or a technique that you use. That doesn't make you terrible at everything you do. It simply means that you need to take extra care of few things.

In any professional environment, it is important to accept positive and negative criticism with open mind. If you're willing to accept appreciation, then you have to listen to your weaknesses.

Chapter 4

Challenge Yourself

In every organisation, the salesperson will come across a question, perhaps on a daily basis.

"Where is the order"

Unfortunately, most of the businesses can be monotonous, causing even the best of sales professionals to fall into patterns that annihilate them of their potential.

In this chapter, we will discuss ways to engage the salesperson fight monotony. We will also find ways to keep them fresh and performing at their best.

Break Patterns: Everyone likes to keep things easy and hence patterns are formed to ease the work. These patterns could be anything eg opening remarks, presentations, preparation. We may even fall into a pattern while demonstating or presenting product/services features or benefits. It is like working in autopilot mode; thereby limiting our abilities to adapt to situations or customer behaviors.

Therefore, a true salesperson must challenge themselves to remain innovative and try different approaches. Hence saleperson should do these things:-

1. Try 2 to 3 different sales pitch to present your product, process, feature or benefit to the customer.

Practices

2. To look for new stories and analogies on which you can base your work and sales pitch.

While trying these different approaches on set of a targeted audience, see which gathers better response. The key here is to get a few more closure every month with a simple change in approach, so let's give it a try.

Be Likeable: We prefer to deal with people we like. Therefore being likeable is like "a connection," but you have to stay likeable from the start of communication till the end. Being likeable means you need to be nice, respectful, enthusiastic, confident and most importantly authentic. You naturaly become likeable when you are seen as dependable. In this era, salespeople cant be just fine actors. You need to be yourself. You also have to standby your customer. Please make sure that you're doing it with a smile.

Deliver More Value: Always, The key to sales is to deliver more value than what the prospect is expecting.

Pre-Sales: Many salespersons don't like to share complete information as they fear that they might loss control over customer or they might get used. This belief actually holds them back and they form a pattern where they block themselves from being likeable. This eventually results into a state where they might not be creating enough value to comfort the prospect feel appreciative to do business with them. Remember, the key to sales is to provide more value than what the prospect is expecting.

Post Sales: You can win a customer for life, if you deliver even 1% more than what you commit. What does delivering atleast 1% more means? It can be better quality product, It may be improved delivery periods or perhaps enhance warranty or AMC. You can expect several references from such a satisfied customer.

Understand Competitive Landscape: Market is now widely open with all kind of marketing, digital marketing and social media marketing. Hence be prepared and updated when a prospect brings up competitor references, use it as one of the great opportunities you have to build value and close business.

So, what sources are your customers using to get their information? Primarily from competitors salesperson, nextly internet, reference from other users. Therefore understanding where they are coming from will take you half way through. You will be able to close the deal by understanding the competitive landscape and selling for and against consumer perceptions.

Follow Up: Always remember that **80% of prospects say no four times before agreeing to a sale.**

The mystifying thing about follow-up is that we all know the benefits, yet many salespersons fail in the consistent and systematic execution of this basic yet critical sales practice. A Salesperson can win additional business every month by simply not giving up on a customer.

Customers too prefer salespersons who are visible and audible to them. This visibility and audibility creates a sense of obligation. This obligation can actually become a tool for selling more. The point is to focus on staying available.

Just make sure you have something to say other than asking the customer if he or she has made a decision yet.

Finally, Challenge yourself to learn from failures.

Every once in a while, when you attempt something new, you may fail. "It is important to pick yourself up from failures and learn from them. Don't be afraid to experiment, don't be afraid to learn

Practices

from setbacks and use those lessons as stepping stones for the future."

Everybody talks about game changers in our business, but you don't need a game changer. What you really need is incremental business that is predictable and sustainable. So challenge yourself to make it happen.

Part II

Productivity

Chapter 5

Be Self Disciplined

"We don't have to be smarter than the rest; we have to be more disciplined than the rest." -Warren Buffett

Self-discipline is the ability to plan and execute it. It means that you do what you should be doing. Self-discipline often means coming out of comfort zone and working on long term goals.

Self disciplined people are self motivated and achieve satisfaction in life. Therefore practising self discipline enables them to move ahead in their profession. People who follow self discipline religiously achieve longterm goals, decrease anxiety, increase physical health, positively impact relationships, become more resilient and feel happier.

The ways to build Self-Discipline

1. Identify your weakness

Many people don't know, what they don't know. As a conscious individual, you must always know what you don't know. Once you know your weakness, you will find a solution or alternative. Therefore you may see that everyone is struggling at something. Start by recording your daily activities by end of the day. Then, review on where you spent most of your time. Then ask yourself whether your behaviors uphold those activities. There are likely a few things you're doing each day that don't honor your values.

After you have identified your weaknesses, try to get feedback from your colleagues, mentors and family who know you best. Try to find out if there is overlapping between how others see you and how you identify yourself.

Once you've recognised in on a few weaknesses, put up an action plan, such as, "One of my areas of improvement is to procrastinate calling prospects until it's too late in the day. This puts me behind for the rest of the week and makes it tough to meet the target. Tomorrow, I'm going to make "X" number of calls first thing when I get to the office."

2. Look for ways to enhance productivity

In any organisation, you will see a morning pattern i.e. colleagues Greeting each other and asking about their evenings. A trip to the kitchen for coffee. Team lunch. An afternoon walk to the local coffee shop.

You may notice that all of these small trips add up to a lot of time away from work. It's important to build relationships with coworkers and give yourself mental and physical breaks throughout the day.

But it's also important to realise that productivity is lost due to such patterns. If your mornings are consumed by non-work-related events and that's when you're most efficient – that's not a good thing. Know when you do your best work and schedule around it.

If you're most dialed in from 9:00 a.m. to 12:00 p.m., schedule those coworker coffee breaks for the afternoon. Protect your ability to perform at work. You'll promote a better environment for yourself and improve results for your company.

3. Set clear goals

In order to achieve self-discipline you must have a clear idea of what you want to accomplish. You should clearly identify what success means to you and those should become your Goals.

Do you know you're 42% more likely to achieve your goals if you write them down? The act of writing down goals empowers you to visualize the goal itself, how to accomplish it, and what steps you should take to get there.

Therefore, when you set out to become the best version of yourself – whether at work or in your personal life – identify your goals and write them down.

4. Visualize the outcome

Our brain can't differentiate between real and imagined memories. Hence, when we imagine something vividly, our brain chemistry changes as if we'd actually experienced it.

Imagine that when you make it or accomplish your goal, you are going to treat yourself with an excellent dinner and that gives you a affirmative feeling of outcome. These feelings will reduce fear and insurities. This will enable you to be more action oriented leaving all kind of fears and insecurities behind. Thus converting visualisation into actionable steps.

5. Now is the right time

If you keep waiting for your plan to be perfect, your desk to be clear, or your inbox to reach a manageable level, you might never get started. It also means that you have added a layer of procrastination on the work that needs to be done. Hold every moment as having just what you need to do your best work. Now is the best time to start doing it.

6. Get Started

The most important part is getting started. You know your goals. You know your weaknesses. You are inspired to be the ideal salesperson. Start small.

Always remember that fixing your work habits in one week is a recipe for stress and disaster.

However pick up a small habit to focus on each week. For week one, you may decide to bring your coffee to the office to avoid the morning break in favor of getting right to work.

With a week of success, you might add a few hours on your calendar every Friday afternoon to finish up administrative tasks like adding prospect notes to the CRM or replying to outstanding emails. After a few weeks of improving one habit at a time, you might surprise yourself with how much more productive and self-disciplined you've become.

7. Identify a mentor

There are things you can discuss with a mentor when you might not be comfortable approaching a colleague or manager. If you want to stop wasting much time on social media; when you are supposed to be prospecting, you may feel better bringing that challenge to your mentor rather than your boss.

Mentors generally have more experience, know you well and can give you the unvarnished advice and feedback you need to succeed – not just in your job but in your career with respect to your Goals.

8. Practice, fail, start over

Acomplishing self discipline doesn't mean that you will never spend an hour on social media and lose few prospects before

10:30 am. It means that you are conscious of what you did (out of whatever reasons) and make sure that next morning you will try to make better decisions.

Self-discipline is the act of trying, failing, and trying again.

9. Measure progress periodically

When you have defined a path and timeframe, it becomes more important to check achievements at regular intervals. Without a system of tracking progress, it will be difficult to know if you are succeeding.

If your goal is to book more orders during the first half of the month, start by identifying how many orders you want to book. Then, work backward to figure out how many orders you'll need each week and how long each one will take to finalize.

Once you've determined the details of your goal, decide what success looks like. Are you simply shooting for the overall number? Will it count if an order is cancelled at the last minute? Should the order lead to a demo? Determine what success looks like, so you know how to measure it.

10. Love yourself

Self-discipline is not worthy if you're killing yourself to achieve it. Everyone works the occasional double shift or perhaps triple shift, but if you're burning the midnight oil for weeks or months to be more "self-disciplined," you've missed the plot.

Part of self-discipline is taking care of yourself. Breaks throughout the day, a healthy diet, plenty of sleep and healthy relationships make the world and us go around. In fact, studies show mindfulness exercises like taking a short walk, noticing five things around you, or identifying two smells can actually increase productivity in the workplace.

11. Reward yourself

It is important to celebrate small accomplishments. It can be exciting to plan a reward for yourself when you achieve a milestone. It is similar to old times when you were a kid and got treated for good results. Having something to look forward, gives you the motivation to succed.

"You have earned this"

"You deserve this"

If you want good habits to stick then rewarding yourself is the key. Deficit means we start justifying bad behaviors and it's often the start of the end of our progress.

Anticipation is powerful and so give yourself treats throughout your self-discipline practice. It gives you something to obsess over and focus on. These treats, whether a nice dinner or a new pair of shoes, will help you feel energized, restored, and never deprived.

Finally when you achieve your goal, find a new set of goals and new rewards to keep yourself motivated and moving upwards.

12. Forgive yourself

Once again, Self-discipline is the act of trying, failing, and trying again.

Holding yourself responsible for failure will derail the whole journey and bring you to a stand still position yet again. You must forgive yourself when you slip. Failure is inevitable, but it is not final.

Be realistic, consider this

If you wake up late, rush to the office and forget to bring your coffee which thrusts you into a 30-minutes break to fetch coffee and that you are three prospect calls short of your daily goal, look at the situation realistically.

Did you fail to meet your goal? Yes. Will you have to make a few more calls tomorrow? Probably. Will this have any effect on your longterm progress? Nope. Once you've looked at the impact of your slip, you can decide how to move forward and get back on track. Step one? Make sure your alarm is set before going to bed.

The key is to keep moving, don't let yourself down in guilt, anger or frustration because these emotions will only drag you further down. Learn from your missteps and forgive yourself.

Remember, self-discipline is a practice. You will not be perfect every day. What's important is showing up each day ready to try.

Chapter 6

Goal Setting

Goal Setting is a tremendous task and is definitely not an easy one. It depends on so many internal and external factors that sometimes it can feel like playing blind. These factors when come into play, can help or hinder your capability to strive for the targets.

One of the biggest mistake goal setter makes most of the time is to solely focus on the numbers. Everyone wants to drive more sales and achieve more profitable business. However without a plan, goals are just dreams.

"Therefore, Fail to Plan is Planning to fail"

Things to consider while preparing goals.

1. Vision & Mission along with long-term goals of your company.

2. In an attempt to hit target, sales can pursue bad, unprofitable, and risky deals. This can have serious implications for the company.

3. Over-promise and under-deliver is the worst thing salesperson can do.

We want the numbers we finalise those to be M.A.P. (Motivating, Achievable and Practical). As we know, If salespersons feel that their targets are unreasonable, then they will tend to be counterproductive.

Hence we use S.M.A.R.T methodology for Goal setting.

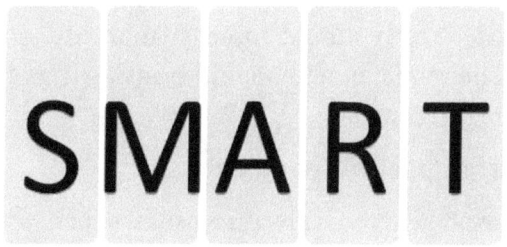

Specific

Measurable

Achievable

Realistic

Time-based

Any goal, which can't be validated on the above points need to be reconsidered. This should be used as ultimate checklist for validation of planned Goals & Targets. Finally, we want these goals to motivate our sales team to exceed expectations and drive business towards new levels.

Finalising sales targets - bottoms up!

Setting a sales figure without considering a plan of action can be unreasonable and result into waste of time, efforts and resources. It is important to challenge the sales team to meet targets but targets need to be realistic and aligned with final goal.

"Build a bottoms up forecast to get visibility into the business, then set a stretch goal on top. A target should feel ambitious but achievable - as a guide, feeling 80% confident hitting your number is about right'. This approach is centered around assessing your current situation and capabilities to see what you can reasonably achieve from there." - Tom Pepper, Director of Marketing Solutions at LinkedIn

Thus the sales team should forecast monthly, quarterly and yearly sales. The management should translate this forecast into sales goals for the team.

Use data from past to set goals

Data from pervious year is always a useful benchmarking source, as it acts as yardstick to growth and profitability. Therefore, we should use it carefully to our advantage. We can find out historic growth rates and past performance of the best salesperson, regions and even competitors.

We also need to divide the target into segment of activities which need to be focused to achieve the desired sales. Therefore the Goal is not just to get the number, the goal is to accomplish each of these activities which effect the performance.

When we work backwards from company's annual sales target, it gives realistic view of the activities that need to be performed in order to achieve the desired outcome.

Let's do some quick calculation with a salesperson goal-setting example.

Review a salesperson's past performance and find out how many calls, emails or sales meetings they typically required to close a deal.

Say, it takes them 10 calls to make a sale and their close rate is 10%. Thus, we can calculate how many calls they need to hit their target.

Let us say their target is 50 deals this year, this transforms to making 500 calls. 500 calls annually divide into almost 40 calls per month or further down 10 call per week.

Dividing your sales goal into smaller monthly/ weekly/ daily goals will help you analysis the facts faster. This will create a sense of responsibility with attention to details toward the goal. It will also create a sense of urgency for sales team whenever they see that their target is lagging behind on monthly basis.

Hence, setting smaller targets can help us achieve bigger goals.

"You may not be able to control the outcome, but can definetly control the actions and inputs of the process".

Educate and empower your sales team

Many of the organisation focus primarily on the sales revenue as yardstick for Sales Goal setting. This in turn monopolize the sales-team focus and when salesperson try to achieve those by tricks and tactics, it can have serious consequences in future.

A Sales Goal should inspire the sales team to sell more and better. Therefore, understand from them about their strengths, weaknesses, and the areas they are looking to improve. You may get lot of valuable feedback like improving product demos, improving marketing plan, building confidence with down the line executives.

Always, set aside a fixed amount of time to coach sales-team and set targets to help them accomplish their personal and professional goals. This will give them a feeling and belief system that you value them enough to invest in them.

"A motivated team will always deliver the strongest and best performance in the long run".

How to crash your sales goals

We must strive on the need to take time to plan and build our strategy in advance.

As Abraham Lincoln said, "If I had 8 hours to chop down a tree, I would spend 6 of those hours sharpening my axe". Sales persons who religiously plan, and then work towards the plan, always exceed their targets.'

Plan for failure - it happens

Thorough planning doesn't just comprise looking at what you have to achieve i.e. your goals, it also examines the gaps and the roadblocks which you might encounter during your course.

Sales Manager don't set targets to fail but the obstracles are an inescapable part of business.

Therefore evolving a proactive plan to deal with gaps and obstacles puts you in a powerful position to troubleshoot rapidly. Your plan need not be exhaustive. Just follow this quick process.

Focus your goals around the actions you can take to empower your sales people to hit their targets.

Therefore getting the right system in place to facilitate simple pipeline management and successful selling, should be top priority.

Prioritize goals

Activity-based goals let's salespersons to win back control, but there is another important aspect to it and that is prioritising these goals.

Establish the goals which generate the highest value or make the most impact and motivates you focus on your energy accordingly. This should include activities that matter the most to your professional goals and the company's bottom line.

Appreciate and Reward performance

The Manager should always recognise the efforts made by sales-person to achieve their goals. You should also think about the ways to acknowledge smaller activity-based goals and milestones like customer service and satisfaction. This will encourage sales-person to sign off on the right customers and focus their attention on the customer satisfaction.

Celebrating quick closes that don't transform into long term customers isn't good sign for the sales team, or the business.

Stretching the Goal

As discussed earlier, setting realistic targets is essential for sales-team morale. According to experts the practise of stretch goals is an important tactic to achieve success.

"Set a stretch goal above your target, think big and be ambitious."

Sales managers should establish stretch goals for themselves and the team. There's nothing wrong in encouraging and engaging your team to exceed expectations and strive for more.

Results are always reviewed and performance is appreciated by the management in form of promotions and bonuses.

Sales targets are fundamental to success

Sales professionals are evaluated on results, so steady performance is the key to success. It's also important to review the efforts and the approach a sales person has; as results are sometimes down to other factors. If you continue to develop your plan and accomplish effectively, the outcome will be desireable.

Goal Setting

Without clear goals, sales-persons are likely to lose enthusiasm and momentum. This will have a substantial impact on the performance and thus the sales.

By setting a clear objective, you provide something for sale-persons to attempt towards and level performance against.

Successful sales managers are dynamic, thus they are flexible with their strategy and use data to generate to align and re-align their sales goals accordingly.

That's how you can set smarter goals that you and your team can consistently achieve.

Setting goals that are both challenging and attainable will motivate your team to strive for greatness and in turn, drive long term success for the business.

S	Specific	What do you want to accomplish?
M	Measurable	How will you know when you have accomplished your goal?
A	Attainable	Is it realistic and attainable?
R	Relevant	Is this goal worth working hard for? Explain
T	Time-specific	By when the goal will be accomplished?

Chapter 7

Time Management

"Time is money." We all know this phrase. Unlike a technican, designer or any other professional, you as a salespersons aren't paid fixed amount for the hours they put in. They are paid or rewarded for the results i.e. sales. The more you sell, the more money you make. Therefore their time really is money.

Many people wish to have 28 hours in a day, for them there aren't enough hours in the day. However actual problem may not be lack of time but how we use it. Using time effectively is important to sales success and it is also one of the biggest challenges. In this chapter we will learn to free few extra hours daily.

A salespersons need to perform various activities which are productive, non-productive, essential and non-essential and then judged by results alone. You are being pulled in different directions and struggling distractions.

As you will not be able to add hours to your day but cutting or delegating non productive and non-essential activities can help you add more hours to your day. And this is the most useful skill a salesperson should learn as soon as possible. This will result in increasing focus and productivity thereby boosting success.

1. Track Your Time

The first thing to do when it comes to time management is to figure out and list down how you spend your day. We are unaware of the habits that kill our productivity. If you are always in a situation where you feel that you have too much to do and very less time to do it in, then the best way to take control of such situation is to accept and understand your working pattern.

If you spend a lot of time online then consider using following apps for self-monitoring:

1. Toggl App : Try tracking specific tasks using Toggl.

2. RescueTime App: To push you back toward productivity.

3. Pomodoro app: This app can help if hurrying and resting suit your workflow.

After a fortnight, we should see some patterns surfacing. We should do a thorough analysis of your log to figure out where we can be more productive and adjust activities accordingly.

2. Start monitoring progress of S.M.A.R.T. Goals

We have already discussed S.M.A.R.T Goals i.e. **S**pecific, **M**easurable, **A**chievable, **R**ealistic, **T**ime-based. People who set their goals and monitor progress of those goals, perform 30% better than those who don't. Setting smart goals increase motivation and achievement. The probability of accomplishing goal becomes very high, when goal is specific.

Setting goals is incomplete without regular review. 360 degree feedback is also an important tool to consider. Watching your progress will reflect how much you have achieved and what correction/ improvement needs to be made.

3. Apply 80/20 rule.

Most of the Managers and Salesperson would be familiar with 80/20 rule. 20% of our time produces 80% of our results. Hence, one should focus on essential and productive tasks rather than non essential and non productive ones. Non essential and non productives can be eliminated or outsourced.

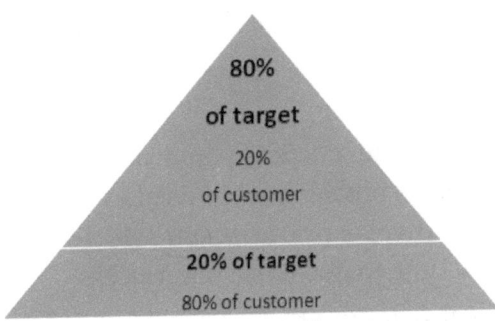

There is another way of applying this Pareto Principle of 80/20. 80% of our sales come from 20% of our customers. That's true for the business, however many of salespersons will have names on their list that will never buy and others have a list that will become high value, long term clients. Therefore classify the leads as soon as possible.

4. Set Appointments in Batches.

When you set an appointment outside the office, do consider who else you could meet in that locality. However, last minute meetings or unscheduled appointment will make you waste a lot of productive time. Map your market and meet with prospects. You should make sure that you catch up with your current customers within the same territory.

When you efficiently and effectively manage your travel between appointments, you can meet with more influencers and prospective buyers, increasing your sales potential.

5. Stop Multitasking

Many of us believe that multitasking brings in more productivity, however studies have shown that multitasking actually slows us down. Our brain can't do two things at one time.

When we think we're multitasking, our brain is actually rushing from one task to another in quick succession. As a result, we lose 40% productivity because the brain is constantly shifting gears and trying to focus.

Multitasking kills our efficiency and performance. It can be even more harmful as probability of mistakes increases. Hence, it becomes essential that we prioritize our sale-activities and focus on one thing at a time to maximize our success.

6. Grouping Similar Tasks

Making batch of similar tasks together leads to greater productivity and efficiency. Allocate specific amount of time each day for cold calling, return calls at same time each day rather than continously checking your voicemail.

Assign an hour or two in the afternoon toward prospecting for the following day. Ensure that you adhere to the schedule, hence once the time is up, move on to the next task. Scheduling activities this way advances your workflow because when you concentrate on one activity at a time, you become more productive, quick and more accurate.

7. Find Qualified Leads Faster

It is importact to understand and accept that not every prospect will be a buyer and not every buyer will buy from you. If your market share is 15% then most important task for you is to identify set of 25 to 30% of the market which has your 15% share.

Being a salesperson and spending time with a wrong prospects cab cost you an opportunity, which you could have spent and nurtured in that amount of time. Most likely, you will have a system to identify qualified leads but it can be hard to let go of a potential sale, even one that appears to have less chance. However, disqualifying leads as quickly as possible allows you to move on to ones that are more likely to become customers. So view a 'NO' as a good thing.

8. Follow: The 2-Minute Rule

Don't procrastinate if it takes just 2 minutes to complete a task. If you can finish it in 2 minutes, then just do it now.

We are all subject to completion bias, which means that we like the feeling of ticking task off a list. So if we make our whole day about lists, it's easy to tick off a bunch of easy stuff, feel a sense of accomplishment and then look back on the whole day wasted on busy work. However many small, simple tasks simply don't deserve the energy that's spent on them to enter them into the system. These small and simple tasks look big once we start treating those like projects.

"If something comes up in the day and it just takes a couple of minutes, don't schedule it: just do it".

9. Avoid Distractions

We are surrounded with people, news, activities and therefore there can be serveral reasons which will be leading to distractions each and every day. As a result we lose our focus from our goals. A minute here or there may seem small but it all adds up over the course of the full day.

Planning our day in advance is the best way to fight distractions. Therefore, find time to plan things, set priorities and stay focus on those.

Time Management

Tips: Set your phone out of sight unless it is unavoidable.

Although social media has become an important element of the sales process, spending 15 minutes checking updates and newsfeeds can easily turn into an hour wasted by browsing funny videos.

As mentioned above, use productivity apps to control and monitor social media usage.

10. Take Short Breaks:

Taking short breaks in between work leads to a healthy and productive style of working. The simple act of taking a break improves your focus and enhances your efficiency. Giving yourself a break away from the desk for as little as 10 minutes; will help you clear your mind and improve your concentration. When you return to your computer, you will feel refreshed and ready to handle your next task more efficiently.

11. Priortise:

Takeaway:

Finally, the key to time management for the busy and always occupied salesperson is to work smarter, not just harder. Get free from distractions, prioritize and focus on most important task: i.e. selling. When you manage your time rather than letting it manage you, you'll be less stressed and more effective, productive and successful.

		High Urgency	Low Urgency
High Importance		Action: **Do first**	Action: **Do next** (or schedule)
Low Importance		Action: **Do latter** (or delegate)	No Action **Don't Do it**

How important is the task? (y-axis) How Urgent is the Task? (x-axis)

Chapter 8

Sales Mindset

"You were born a winner, a warrior, one who defied the odds by surviving the most gruesome battle of them all - the race to the egg. And now that you are a giant, why do you even doubt victory against smaller numbers and wider margins? The only walls that exist are those you have placed in your mind. And whatever obstacles you conceive, exist only because you have forgotten what you have already achieved."

— *Suzy Kassem*

The tools, techniques or sales skills might not be holding you back from realizing your full potential. It may be your own thinking about selling and confidence in your personal sales abilities that creates undesirable hindrances in your path to selling success. Your sales mindset impacts all aspects of your sales performance.

In any organisation, may it be a Public Limited or a Private Limited or even a Properiotorship business, everyone is selling whether you think so or not. Every day you get up, dress up and go to sell yourself, your product or service to make your business grow.

If you're not sure about your success probability in selling, consider the following 13 personality traits anticipated to create a superstar sales mindset.

Productivity

1) Stay Motivated

Every good salesperson you encounter will be self-driven. They always have high energy level and a strong work ethic. They work harder and longer than their co-workers. When the economy is slow, they work even harder looking for ways to reach out prospects more effectively. They are always hungry.

2) Honesty is the best policy

A true professional needs to be sincere, hence you must never compromise your integrity.

Truth always prevail, so telling the truth is the best policy, especially in current business scenario, it's a must. A few years back, the Forum Corporation in Boston studied 341 salespeople from 11 different companies across different industries. Their aim was to establish what separated the top performer from the average performer.

When the research finished, the results were startling. It was not skill, knowledge or personality that divided the pack. The difference came down to one trait: honesty. When customers trust you, they buy from you.

3) Attitude matters

It is your attitude, not your aptitude that will determine your altitude. Your positive attitude can make the difference to your personality.

Sales happens in the mind first. We can alter our life by altering our mind. In tough economies, it may not be our fault for being down but it is certainly our fault for not getting up and selling aggressively. Success is 90 percent mental. We have to be a believer to be an achiever.

Hence, stay positive.

4) Be authoritatian

Sales superstars know their products inside-out, upside-down. They also know what is available in market i.e. competitors' product and their key selling features. Hence, they are prepared to point out the differences very clearly.

5) Get prepared

Salesperson like a soldier should always be prepared. Being prepared here means upto date with your product and with your market. Make sure S.M.A.R.T. goals are getting aligned and accomplished along the timeline.

The Soldier's slogan says, "Be always prepared." Absolutely, it's true. It takes a lot of discreet preparation to yield outstanding results.

6) Mind your reputation.

Reputation is earned with time and you definitely can't order a reputation. Reputation leads to referencing i.e. Positive reference and Negative reference.

Before taking a favourable decision any customer will do a reference check about product quality and company's service support. If you don't have positive references and customers swearing by you then it will be a hard task for you to sell your product. Therefore, always care for your reputation.

7) Likeability matters.

Genuine people are liked by most of the people because they don't misguide and they aim for long term relationships rather than short term gains.

They are easy to reach out for any kind of need as they are pleasant. We always like to deal with people we like.

8) First Impression matters

Many times you will not get a second chance in life. Hence, you have to do your best right in the first meeting. Dress up like a professional and follow your organisation's policy on dressing. Be neat and well groomed as that adds to self confidence.

9) Set goals.

We have already discussed S.M.A.R.T Goals i.e. **S**pecific, **M**easurable, **A**chievable, **R**ealistic, **T**ime-based goals. Setting smart goals increase motivation to achieve those. The probability of accomplishing goal becomes very high, when goal is specific.

10) Be Customer Service Oriented

We often come across sayings like "Customer is King", "Customer is God", "Customer is the read boss", "Customer is foremost important person" and so on.

A Customer relationship begins when the customer says "YES". The salespeople must make sure that the job is done on time and done as commited. Every business is always looking for more sales, which means they are always looking for customers. A delighted customer will tend to sell for you. Hence, be customer service oriented and give attention to all the details.

11) Listen carefully

Pay attention to details. The most important part of sales is to listen and understand customer's requirement. If you miss out a small detail then that can cause you lot of embaressment and even financial loss to your business. Good listening doesn't mean "I talk, you listen."

Communication is a two way process. Eventually listening is more important than talking because you don't know what your ears might miss to listen. If you talk to customers instead of hearing to them, they're not buying in but perhaps they're caving in.

12) Keep learning and improving

Learning is a continuous lifelong process, therefore one should develop a longing for learning and self improvement. Top salespersons constantly work on upgrading their skills through formal and non formal courses. Apart from taking courses, they read books, listen to podcasts and inhale everything they can to enhance their game.

Top performing salespersons, while selling have moved beyond telling and explaining. We will learn in one of our next chapter "Telling isn't Selling."

Part III

Preparation

Chapter 9

Become the Product Expert

"If you can become the product expert with whom everyone wants to consult, then you are at a completely different level of selling."

A salesperson is expected to know his product well enough to answer all the queries raised by prospective customers. Inspite of product trainings, we have seen about 75% of salespersons and early managers when asked further details on specific product features, there come out with replies like this "We will get back to you."

If a customer goes back with such an answer (We will get back to you) then you have but naturally lost his confidence. Further, if you don't get back to him in specified time then you will lose the customer completely.

Hence, it is important that the salesperson answers all the doubts raised by the prospective customer as precisely as possible. Salesperson must be able to clearly communicate the features and benefits of things they are selling, thereby driving the value realisation for the customer.

Need for becoming product expert:

In this era when there are multitude sellers, buyers have more choices than ever before. Therefore these choices confuse the

Become the Product Expert

buyers and complicates the buying process.

If the salesperson become a product expert, this will simplify and shorten the buying process, as he can clarify and handle customer's objections instantly. Customers might want to know how you control quality of your product and processes. They might as well be interested in the product testing stages i.e. testing, modification and retesting.

Technical specification and Performance data are important for most of the prospective customers. Many of them are proactive about product maintenance or AMC, therefore they can have genuine query about spares and serviceability.

Further a Salesperson should be able to provide accurate price and delivery information about the products. A smart salesperson will also be able to get product data for competition products too, for comparison purpose.

A proposal containing ROI (Return on Investment) data gets a lot of attention and appreciation thereby enabling you to get favourable response especially in case of Industrial or Commerical selling. For the customer, you are the point of contact for business so be prepared to share you company's mission and vision.

One of the easiest way to be a product expert is to try using your own product, see how it performs, discuss with your team and listen to the customer feedback.

Customers don't buy products just for their features but for the value they would get out of it i.e. the benefits.

Be sure to learn everything you can about your products (and those of your competitors) and practice using bridge statements to clearly communicate the features and benefits.

Preparation

As we discover the importance of becoming product expert with complete product knowledge and strategies, it becomes more interesting to find out how do we become the product expert?

Some of the basic things which we can start doing almost immediately are as below:

- Read your own brochures, pamphlets, catalogs and advertisements.

- View you company's presentation and other audio visual material.

- Go for a plant tour to see firsthand how your products are produced.

- Talk to other people in your organization: salespeople, customer service people, delivery people.

- Talk to your customers. Listen to them. Customers being the users know in and out of it.

- Talk to competitor's customer and understand how your product is perceived in the market.

- If possible, try your own products. Using your products and carefully evaluating them will improve your product knowledge and confidence.

Being the product expert will make you a more valuable resource for both your organisation and your customers.

Let's take this case study from Inc.com by Vanessa Merit Nornberg, President, Metal Mafia

Become the Product Expert

"Last week, I went to a butcher shop instead of the supermarket where I usually buy my meats, and a funny thing occurred. I came home with three times the amount of food I had intended to get. How did this happen? Because the man behind the counter was an expert: he not only knew every cut of meat, but also which cut was best for particular dishes— and it did not stop there. He gave me cooking times and temperatures for everything I chose and even recited me a few quick recipes using cuts I was unfamiliar with."

What a change from the supermarket experience where I have to either help myself or am served (rather than sold) by someone other than a specialist! Whether your company offers multiple product lines or just one, the key to sales growth is making sure anyone selling your merchandise is not just a greeter, but a true expert on the products he is being asked to sell.

Hence, it becomes more motivating to turn your sales team into product experts. If not, your customers may be walking out the door empty-handed.

3 Ways to Facilitate Salesperson become Product Experts

1. **Institute Roleplay.**

    Every person in the sales team should be comfortable enough with his products to sell on the spur of the moment. Every Monday, in your weekly sales meeting, either business head or sales head should randomly ask a salesperson to sell you a specific product as though you were a customer. You ask hard questions, raise objections, and force them to think about the product in ways they might not have, if they weren't being put on the spot. And you do this in front of the whole sales team, so that everyone has the chance to listen and learn from one another. Not surprisingly, most people on the team will first draw on the selling points they have been provided on product info sheets. The exercise gets far more interesting, however, when the salesperson starts to think creatively about how and why the product is valuable, drawing on customer feedback, his own experience, or the product's relationship to something else he sells. **Setting up a weekly opportunity to test team members in roleplay scenarios gives the chance to hear where the team lacks knowledge**, and help them to show up their expertise.

2. **Mandatory fieldwork.**

   Salespersons can get a great foundation from training and roleplay, but there is no substitution for getting out in the field and learning firsthand. Take the travel industry as an example. Most consumers have the same tools at their disposal as travel agents do now, thanks to the Internet. Those whose travel businesses continue to prosper despite the do-it-yourself possibilities of web bookings; are agents who specialize in a particular area and who know the secrets of a destination because they have been there themselves and seen up-close the possibilities and pitfalls of the places they are recommending. I used an expert on Thailand to book part of a recent trip, and the best cities we visited and most wonderful places we stayed were those which the specialized salesperson put on our itinerary and not the ones we found ourselves. **Adding experience to information is the single best way to help a salesperson become an expert.**

3. **Encourage explanation.**

   Novice salespersons often think they have to hide the potential drawbacks to their products whereas experts know how to explain them. I recently spent hours doing research on strollers and while I found many that seemed okay, none was perfect. When I headed to a nearby shop, I was happy to find a sales-woman who was able to give me the pros and cons of every stroller available and when we had settled on the one she thought would best fit my needs, she even warned me about two issues owners of this model frequently had trouble with and how to get around them. I was relieved to have finally picked a stroller. Later when I encountered the minor folding and storing issues she had mentioned; I knew how to handle them. No product is perfect, and being able to explain to customers how to make the negative work for them instead of against them, is the last ingredient of becoming a true sales expert.

When product is explained to customer by the expert, it makes their decision making easier. They feel delighted and motivated to buy. Therefore don't simply provide your customers with a salesperson, give them access to the expert. This will also differentiate you from your competitors and as a result you will see increase in your sales and customers will keep coming back to you for more.

Chapter 10

Customer Segmentation

Understanding who is who, "A new way to understand our customers in a structured, shared manner"

At some inflection point of growth, it becomes impossible to instinctively know your customers, let alone decide which ones to focus on.

All customers are unique, they might not have uniform needs and may not be reached the same way. Hence treating all customer alike is like taking them for granted.

Most of the companies mainly rely on the contracts, product performance, sales input and a belief that the customers will stick to them for their product and services. This final assumption in particular is no longer true or useful. Indeed, amongst your customers could be B2C companies, small businesses and large enterprises along with customers in places and industries well beyond a particular geography. All of these customers could be facing entirely different challenges.

You need to find a way to understand your customer's challenges in order to ensure that your solutions solve their problems. Therefore, customer segmentation can help you understand behaviour of set of customers in a structured and shared manner.

Customer segmentation is the exercise of segmenting customers based on common characteristics. These customer groups can be beneficial in marketing campaigns, in identifying potentially profitable customers and in developing customer loyalty.

Customer segments further let you understand the patterns that distinguish your customers. However, collecting data and analyzing it just to understand patterns is useless unless you're going to do something with it. Here are some valuable things you can do with segmentation analysis:

- Identify the most and least profitable customers
- Advance focus marketing efforts
- Improve customer relationship
- Build loyal customers
- Pricing the products differently
- Develop better products
- Customize features

While the type of product and service will determine the customer aspects that are worth segmenting, there are some fundamental characteristics that most organizations should be familiar with and collect data on.

Segmenting customers can seem frightening: where do you start and how do you segment? That answer will depend on your goals and products. However, it will be helpful to think in terms of the 5 W's and an H (who, what, where, when, why and how) while segmenting.

Common types of customer segmentation include:

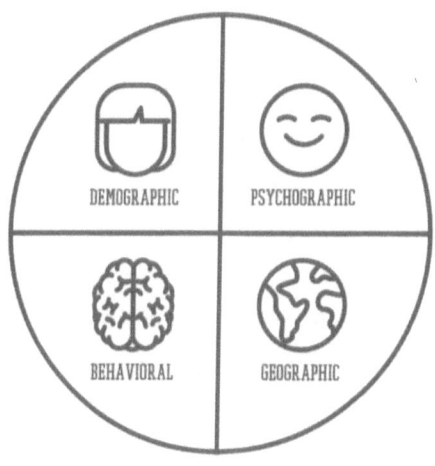

1. Demographic segmentation

2. Psychographic segmentation

3. Behavioral segmentation

4. Geographic segmentation

1. Demographic Segmentation

   Most of marketers agree that audience segmentation is extremely valuable in providing a great customer experience and segment customers based demographic data is one of the most common types of customer segmentation.

A number of parameters you can consider such as age, generation, gender, education, occupation, income, marital status or ethnicity to create customer segments.

It is easier to obtain and measure data for demographic segmentation. A simple way to gather data is to ask your customers or email subscribers to fill out a form.

Case study : NIVEA

NIVEA Sun grew their portfolio to 40 different product variations to meet the requirements of their customers. They used demographic segmentation to segregate their customers and analyze their buying behaviors to create a profitable range of products.

For example, men chose convenience when it comes to suncare products while women chose luxury. The choice of a product also depends on people's occupation because that decides how long they spend in the sun. Using an effective segmentation strategy, NIVEA Sun was able to deliver more value to their customers.

2. Psychographic Segmentation

Alongwith understanding customer preferences and interests, you also need to know which stage of the buying process they are in. This type of customer segmentation is called lifecycle or customer journey-based segmentation.

You can create various segments such as consumers who have visited your online store but haven't made a purchase or customers who have bought only once in the last 12 months or haven't bought in the last 12 months.

Customer journey-based segmentation provides you with a

powerful approach to target them with more relevant and useful references.

3. Behavioral Segmentation

Segmenting customers based on the way they interact with your product and brand is known as Behavioral segmentation.

Perhaps you can create a segment for customers who have added products to their cart but didn't complete the checkout or ones who did not even add any products to their cart but simply browsed. You can also group by products or services they showed interest in.

Some common variables that determine behavior segmentation include:

Occasion: Segmentation based on purchases for a specific occasion such as weddings, festivals, etc.

Usage: Segmentation based on the frequency of their purchases.

Thought Process: Segmentation based on the driving force behind their purchase decisions.

Also, the lack of behavior such as an incomplete survey form allows you to re-engage consumers using personalized messaging.

For example, Online Store like Amazon and Lazada have mastered the art of targeting their customers based on their recent purchases and recently viewed products.

4. Geographic Segmentation

Geographic segmentation comprises grouping customers by country, state, region, climate or market size. You need to adapt your communications to various geographic segments keeping in mind the local culture and rituals.

Amending your offerings and marketing communications for different geographic segments provides greater value to consumers and encourages them to buy. Localisation can help customer relate to the product more quickly.

Benefiting from these Segments:

1. Value each segment

Segmentation will allow you to value each segment of your customer base. This is important, as 80 percent of your sales typically come from only 20 percent of your customers. Identifying those groups that provide the highest volume of sales and quantify the total volumes is very important. These are your high-value segments. You can then use this information to re-align your marketing efforts, prioritize service to this group and adjust your offerings to more closely meet their requirements. Value-based segmentation will help you increase sales revenue.

2. Focus your marketing resources

Understanding your most important segments can allow you to change your marketing efforts to reach those segments more directly. You can customise your advertising language and message to appeal more clearly to them. You can also modify your advertisements for each product-line so that it appeal to the corresponding segments that buy that product-line. *Focused marketing will enable you save on advertising cost.*

3. Prioritize different segments

Segmentation can help you see which customer groups are the

Preparation

most profitable for you. You can more easily see which groups go on to do the most business with you and buy the more expensive items and service packages. You can then compare this to the money you spend marketing to them. This data will allow you to realign your customer prioritization. **Hence prioritizing can increase your profit margin.**

4. Improve your offerings

Once you know exactly who is buying each of your products and services, you can make and offer alternate products and services to better appeal to these groups. These modifications will make the product more useful and more appealing to this group. Consequently this will give you an advantage over your competitors. You may also apply your learnings to your customer services and other products to create a whole new customer experience tailored to a particular segment or segments. **Improving offering specific to segments will increase customer loyalty and satisfaction.**

Finally, Segmentation let's you build the right product, set the right distribution and positioning and match the acceptable sales motion to each customer, while also filtering your segments over time. It's a model that can give anyone at your company an immediate understanding and outlook of your customers.

Chapter 11

Market Penetration

Initially, market penetration was one of the four strategies of the so-called Product Market Expansion Grid, a business analysis technique that provides a framework enabling identification of growth opportunities.

This is better known to the world as the *Ansoff Matrix*, a theory named after its creator, Russian-American mathematician and business manager Igor Ansoff.

Business growth strategies are divided into the four quadrants as shown below. The one involving focus on existing product in existing market is popularly known as **Market Penetration**

Strategy. It aims at increasing your market share in existing market with focus on selling your existing products or services.

Typically, market penetration strategy comes in the picture when you are selling your products in a saturated and highly competitive market.

Every company needs to express themselves to get a share of the market. The problem is that the markets are crowded with several products and occupied by richer and more successful companies. These companies do not want to see new players in their field.

You need market penetration strategy when you are looking at the product market expansion. Therefore, as the current market might be saturated or it may be highly competitive or your current product has low turnaround time, in such a case, you need to consider strategy to increase market penetration thereby increasing the market share.

In this chapter, we look at "***the concept of market penetration***". We will also discuss how to create a market penetration strategy and the benefits it brings.

Again, market penetration strategy is an attempt by a company that is already in the market with an off-the-shelf product to take more business from other market participants.

Market penetration is a business tool to achieve strategic business goal. Although, the fact that the concept of market penetration appeared in the middle of the 20th century, we can still take the most important concepts and adjust them to our present realities.

Let's consider market penetration in more detail because it is perfect for the needs of MSME (Micro, Small and Medium Enterprises) and startups.

So, what do we call a market penetration strategy? Putting it in simple words, it is a strategy that allows a company to take a piece of the marketshare from competitors, no matter how large and strong they are.

Let's discuss the need and outcome of this strategy and look at how exactly it can uplift MSME and startups.

Market Penetration is Indispensable: for quick adoption of a MSME/ Startup's product in the market.

Imagine that a business needs somehow to get a share of the market that has been divided among different companies of different sizes. For any business, having its own piece of the marketshare is vitally important as after all this is the only way to achieve consistent and rapid growth.

So how can a company do this?

A marketing penetration strategy helps businesses evaluate the market through quick improvement of their products by knowing the pros and cons of competitors' products.

Any company will also be able to adjust the price of its product to make it attractive for customers. All of this assures getting a customer base relatively quicker and it results in growth of marketshare, thus business.

Many studies and experts confirm that "if your product is cheap enough and of similar quality to competing products, it should spread out into the market and be purchased by customers quickly."

To Drive Competitors out of a Mature Market

If a business declares itself and is able to improve its product and make its price more appealing than those of competitors, it is logical to assume that competitors' customers will gradually move to the company offering an excellent product at a more attractive price.

After all, why should customers pay more if they can save money and still get a product of good quality?

Gradually customers of competitors' bases will switch loyalty to the new and more attractive product. Thus, profits and revenues of mature competing companies may decrease.

This strategy has the ability to help MSME companies to beat the competition.

To Increase Use of a Product by Existing Customers

Implementing out a marketing penetration strategy will also allow the company to consolidate its success.

This can be possible on account of marketing campaign like "special offers" and "loyalty schemes." These two marketing approaches allow already acquired and regular customers of the company to remain pleased through special benefits and discounts for the company's products.

Users of a product also see that a company values them as customers, plus products will be even more attractive for them because of value offered.

Consequently, the company's agitate rate will be low and customer retention rate will be high.

To Scale Your Presence in the Market

This approach may be taken in different ways but it aims at reaching out maximum users and prospects.

The first is to maintain or increase market share by selling a wider scope of products.

Market Penetration

The second way to get a larger market share is to expand your influence in the market. The easiest way to achieve this is to localize your product, software or website to local language/ local advertisement campaign with local endorsements.

Finally to increase the product visibility through more point of sales, digitial marketing and apps based advertisments.

Finally to summarize, market penetration strategy is focusing on selling your existing products or services into your existing markets to gain higher market share.

It is an attempt by a company that is already in the market with an off-the-shelf product to get more sales from other market participants.

The main ways to do this are:

– Improving the existing product to increase its market share and drive out competitors.

– Adjusting the price of the existing product to increase its market share and beat the competition.

– Scaling the presence of the new company within the market.

Chapter 12

The Sales Pitch

A successful sales process isn't implemented overnight. Aside from having a great product, one must also have the tools that are necessary to turn prospects into longterm clients. To attract prospects into your fold, you must be able to convince them that it will be worthwhile to invest in your product or service. You can do this by creating a convincing and compelling sales pitch presentation.

A sales pitch presentation is a short presentation usually done through PowerPoint or Prezi and is an essential tool to close sales faster. If this is the first time you will be creating a sales pitch deck, consider the following formulas to have a successful presentation.

Good sales pitch is more than well-designed set of slides and effective delivery of those slides. The impact of a great sales presentation on moving prospects to buyers; shouldn't be undermined. There are several elements that makes for an effective sales pitch from preparation to delivery to closing for next level. Use the below tips when designing and delivering sales presentation to ensure that you are driving the highest conversion rates possible.

Sales Pitch should have an Objective

Only 20% of salespeople actually understand the objective of their sales presentation, especially given how easy it is to develop an objective. You may be trying to express an overview of your company, your product, and the value proposition you provide to the customers. You may also be trying to learn as much as you can about the prospects, what they need and why they need it. But the most important objective is to use your sales pitch to move the buyer to the next step in your sales process. Your presentation should focus on providing information such as the value you create and what the prospect should do next so that they agree to move on to the next steps with you. It's a simple but often-overlooked point.

Focus on Customer needs

Eye-catching sales presentations provide information on something that prospective customers really care about. Making audience care is the most important thing to do in sales presentation. While creating and ultimately delivering your sales pitch, ask yourself – what's in it for them? There are a number of different business reasons, such as increasing output or saving costs, which would cause a customer to care about your presentation. There can be personal reasons that can be highlighted in presentation that would help prospects to gain recognisation in their industry or organisation as a result of using your product/ services.

Make "achievement" references in the sales pitch

Every good sales presentation is built on top of a success story. As humanbeings we're hardwired to like good examples and in a business setting it's no different. Good stories share a number of

Preparation

common characteristics that can be incorporated into sales pitch. For example, good stories are often personal in nature and induce emotional responses ranging from fear to greed. Customers also like "story arcs" that exhibit how you can implement changes in their organization by changing the status quo. Your sales pitch should show them, how they can get from point A to point B.

A sales pitch should have a organising Idea

Like a story, sales presentation should be organised around a central idea. In most sales presentations that theme should be focused on the benefits that the customer will achieve. As you're creating your pitch ask yourself what's the real benefit you're going to deliver to your buyer. Further make sure that the story you tell in your sales presentation; spins around that benefit.

Sales presentation should be structured

A professional sales presentation should have a structure that makes it easy for the customer to follow what you're presenting. One of the more common structures used in sales presentations is that of articulating what the customer's problem is; presenting a potential solution to that problem and finally agreeing to a next step with the customer. It's a simple structure that allows any prospective buyer to easily follow the presentation. Just remember to keep it simple. Many customers may disagree when you pitch a new idea to them. A smooth flowing presentation can make it easy for them to follow along, thereby helping you overcome that challenge.

Follow 3 X 3 rule in sales presentations

The majority of people can't remember more than three things at a time. Therefore, a good sales presentations should follow a 3×3 rule. The sales pitch should convey information around no more than three big central ideas. Each individual slide should contain no more than three pieces of information that you want the customer to understand.

Sales Pitch Versions : Short & Long

Your sales presentation should have a long and short version.

The long version of your presentation should be approximately 30 to 40 minutes in length and should fill the majority of a 60 minute meeting that you might have with a customer. While the number of slides may vary, it is recommended that target should be two to three minutes per slide. As such, your 30-45 minute sales presentation should have between 15 to 20 slides in it.

The short version of your presentation should be from 10 to 15 minutes in length. Many salespeople wonder why they need a short sales presentation, but there can some situations where a short presentation comes in handy. For example, a customer may tell you that they only have 20/30 minutes to meet instead of an hour you originally scheduled. Short version of your presentation may have slides as few as 5 slides. Moreover, you need to be prepared to give the short version without slides.

Be ready for pitching without slides

The best salespersons are able to deliver their sales pitch without slides. To do this, you need to be an expert or need to practice your pitch without the aid of slides. Focus on the overall structure of your pitch and the story you're trying to tell. You should also practice answering the 5-10 most common questions you get from prospects. Sales pitches that don't use slides tend to turn into conversations much faster (which is a good thing in sales). These conversations usually center around a set of commonly asked questions that you need to be proficient at answering.

Sales pitch should be personalised

The most effective sales presentations are ones with content that is personalized for target audience. There are some simple guidelines that can be followed to minimize the amount of work that's required to customize a presentation for a specific meeting.

Firstly, make sure that only handful of slides are personalized, usually the first few slides in the presentation deck. Secondly, focus on a handful of common ways to include buyer-specific information in the sales presentation. You may include industry specific information or content that is specific to the buyer's role. Further this may also be done by including information collected during need assessment or discovery phase of your sales cycle. Finally; make sure that you have a process for personalizing the presentation prior to the meeting. Many salespersons jump right into their sales pitch without having put any thought into personalization. Make sure that you allocate 15 to 20 minutes before every major sales pitch for personalisation so that you can tell a compelling story to the customer.

Set a Clear Sales Presentation Agenda

At the start of your meeting, set a clear agenda that outlines the structure of the meeting and presentation for the customer. Focus on 3-5 key topics that you want to cover in the sales pitch and put them in a structured order. Always try to time the topics to be covered in the meeting. Long agenda's with confuse the customer and lead to unproductive meeting. Finally, at the end of the meeting always sum-up and if possible make minutes of meeting.

Be specific in sales pitch

A lot of sales presentations are filled with high level information, platitudes, business jargon and vacuous leadership. The sales pitch needs to include specific information that enables the customer to make a better decision which establishes your credibility and credentials, thereby moving the prospect further along in the buying process. Try to include specific information that shows a deep understanding of the target customer, the specific ways you help companies like the customer's and exactly how people use these product or service.

Use authentic examples in sales presentations

The sales presentation should incorporate specific examples and data into your sales pitch. For example, instead of generally describing about your product features, provide the customer with a specific example of how a company from the similar industry uses the product. Whenever possible use contextually relevant examples and specific matrix to support the key points.

Sales presos to be a medium of conversation

Most of the sales presentations focus exclusively on serving the seller communicate information to the customer. However, the most effective sales presos facilitate a two-way exchange of information between seller and buyer. Ensure that your presentation prompts the prospects to share information with you about why they are considering you, their needs and where they are in the buying process. A few simple rules go a long way here, let the customer interrupt you. Moreover. encourage the prospects to enquire by asking them if they have any questions every five minutes. Then present the information that would cause the buyer to either agree or ask more.

Make sure that you leave at least five minutes at the end of the meeting to get feedback from the customer and discuss next steps.

Sales presentation is complete, when it leads to next level

Preparation

One of the most important thing is to reach an agreement to the next step with the buyer at the end of your sales pitch. Explicitly ask the buyer to take the next step with you, whether it's signing the buyer up for trial, scheduling a demo or agreeing to put together a proposal. Actually the entire pitch process is about building to the point where prospect takes the next step towards finalising the deal.

One need to focus on two things to achieve this during the presentation. First, make sure that the buyer agree that there is a problem or opportunity that he needs help with. Second, use the presentation to establish credibility so that you will actually be able to help with that problem or opportunity.

If you do these two things well, then you have cleared this level of discussion and you should prepare for next level which will lead to closing.

Part IV

Prospecting

Chapter 13

Marketing Tools

Marketing creates an opportunity of exchange between business and its customers. Sometimes that exchange transforms into an immediate sale, and at other times it builds awareness of the brand for when future purchases are made.

Role of Marketing

Some of the most essential role of marketing in making a brand or product successful are as follows:

The ***needs pre-exist in market***. They (marketers) identify the needs of the buyer and adopt their strategies accordingly. They influence the wants, as these are shaped by traditional and individual personalities. Their needs are fulfilled through the exchange process.

A business sustains because of customer retention and consistency in the market share. Marketing helps companies achieve their goals because it is customer-centric. Marketing aims at ***satisfying customers beyond their expectations.***

They use communication tools such as advertising, sales, promotion, event marketing and PR to ***promote their products far and wide***. Furthermore, PR programmes shape and enhance a company's brand image. Media technology has made marketing more interactive.

Many companies offer more than one product. Physical products that is goods need to be well packed and labelled. On the other hand services are categorised as intangible and inseparable. Therefore marketing plays an active role by **designing and handling product offerings.**

The product/ services demand can be a negative demand, no demand, latent demand, declining demand, irregular demand, full demand or overfull demand. Hence **demand management** is another key role of marketers. They need to access and influence, level, time and composition of demand. Marketing helps in dealing with these varied levels of demand.

In modern world **competitive positioning** is essential. Thus balancing buyers' expectations and competitors' offering becomes an important role of marketing. This is achieved product differentiation and regular review of product performance. This also calls for monitoring the market closely to retain the market share.

Increasing customer expectations, statutory requirements and environmental degradation have pushed companies to practice higher levels of social responsibilities. Hence **social marketing plays an important role.** Cause-related marketing is commonly used by big corporate houses.

Companies use various marketing tools to communicate business information, stimulate customer interest and prompt action. An integrated marketing approach applies several tools to engage customers and build business.

Companies normal choose their marketing tool based on their marketing goals and the budget. There are primarily following four types of marketing tools available to businesses for promoting their product:

1. Traditional Marketing
2. Digital Marketing
3. Social Media Marketing
4. Promotional Marketing Tools

Traditional Marketing

Traditional marketing make use of media – such as

-billboards,

-banners,

-newspapers,

-magazines,

-television,

-radio and

-telephone,

-directories

-yellow pages

It involve marketing tools such as paid advertisements, commercials and press releases. This approach focuses on sales push and relies on reaching large numbers of people to ensure success.

Marketing through advertising with publications and networks is a costly marketing tool which makes analysing the return on investment particularly important.

Digital Marketing

Information Technology has added lot of aspects to marketing. With more and more usage of computer reaching customers has become easier than before. Computer software technology supports reaching potential customers with targeted, measurable communications. Specific digital media marketing tools include

-S.E.O. search engine optimization,

-mobile marketing,

-interactive online advertisements,

-opt-in email

-Online partnerships such as affiliate marketing and sponsorships.

A key element of digital marketing tools is web analytics, which offer information on an internet user's online activities, IP address and search keywords. This information can then be used to create a targeted advertising campaign to reach business's core audience. To get started in digital media marketing, we may want to hire a digital media marketing agency skilled at bringing a brand to the web's ad networks.

Social Media Marketing

Social media marketing may also be seen as a subset of digital marketing. However, the objective of social media marketing tools is to develop an interactive, online relationship with the customers rather than to mine covertly for customer data. It also leads to reference base with customers rating and recommending company's product and services online.

Specific examples of social media marketing tools include:

-blogging,

-tweeting,

-posting,

-sharing,

-networking,

-pinning,

-bookmarking,

-media sharing and

-commenting on social media

We use social media marketing on websites and app such as following, due to significantly large number of users with these websites and apps:-

-Twitter,

-Facebook,

-LinkedIn,

-Pinterest,

-Reddit and

-YouTube.

Social media marketing tools level the playing field for MSMEs and start-ups by offering low-cost tools with potentially high returns.

Promotional Marketing Tools

Marketing tools includes usage and distribution of promotional items, such as

-brochures,

Marketing Tools

-business cards,

-press kits,

-websites,

-informational videos and

-Merchandise, are tangible marketing tools.

Some of these items include detailed information and highlight attributes of company's products or services. Business cards and trade show giveaways may display only a company logo and provide contact information.

In addition to increasing sales, promotional items contribute to building brand awareness, but cost is a factor when selecting these items.

Chapter 14

Lead Generation

In current modern and rapidly changing business scenario, lead generation plays an important role in closing business. Although lead generation plays a key role in boosting the bottom line however it is also the greatest ongoing challenges.

In this chapter, we'll cover key considerations to keep in mind when developing a lead generation strategy. We'll also explore various techniques for generating leads offline and online.

There might be thousands of prospects out there who are aware of our brand, but until they engage with us in some way, they remain strangers to our company. How do we draw such targets in and capture their interest so that they'll make themselves, and ideally their email addresses or phone numbers, known to us? Through lead generation.

Simply put, lead generation is the process of converting prospects that have indicated an interest in our offering into leads and starting them on the journey of becoming a customer.

After all, if you haven't captured a prospect's interest and figured out how to communicate with them then you have no one to aim your marketing efforts at, no one to develop toward purchase. That's why it's important you manage your lead generation practices well.

Again, we can divide lead generation into two:-

1. Traditional Lead Generation

2. Online Lead Generation

Traditional Lead Generation

1) Cold Calling

As a salesperson, you need to be proactively finding your next lead while leaving an impactful impression. Cold calling might seem like something from the past; however, it is still used today by many salespersons because it does generate leads. However, with cold calling, the roles are reversed and now the agent faces the fear of rejection.

To have a successful cold calling experience, prepare a script that you will present to prospective customers that includes a clear understanding of the product, pricing, market trends and any other information you can use to sell your product or service. This is exceptionally useful for direct selling because preparing a well-versed script will showcase your knowledge and understanding of the product/ services.

Always leave something tangible behind, whether it is a business card, a flyer, or a brochure.

2) Direct Mail

According to researchers, direct mail is on the rise because of the industry's dependence on technology. People are more likely to notice a well-tailored direct mail piece than a standard email. They further suggests creating marketing pieces that interest your client. Good marketing speaks directly to what's on the mind of the consumer.

Prospecting

For previous clients, you might want to reach out to them thanking them for their business. This is also a great time to remind your client to refer you to friends, family, or acquaintances. For potential leads, an area of interest is the value of the product/ services. Create pieces that push clients to ask you about your offerings and eventually ask for a face-to-face meeting in which you can provide them with a product/ service presentation.

3) Networking

A great way to find more leads is to have a wide network of friends, colleagues, and acquaintances. We are not talking about the high school friend you have on Facebook who you send birthday wishes once a year. Create relationships with your network by keeping in touch, sending them cards, and interacting with them during events. By maintaining this level of relationship, whenever an opportunity arises for your friend, colleague, or acquaintance to refer, you will be the first person on their mind.

4) Traditional Advertising

Traditional advertising methods like billboards, bus benches, newspaper ads, and radio advertising slots are still indispensable to many in the industry. A major issue with these forms of lead generation is the high advertising cost. However, a well-placed billboard or radio ad could easily generate thousands of impressions.

When using this form of lead generation, design is a major player. You need to create an ad that will get the attention of those exposed to it. They might not remember it the first time, but by the second or third time the individual will begin to remember what they saw or heard. Make sure to include your name, email, phone number, and website. Create a memorable email address or website URL that individuals can remember after just a couple of impressions.

Modern Lead Generation

1) Website

With so many options in today's online world to generate leads, a company website is by far one of the best ways to drive leads to your business. As the authorized person/ owner of this site, you have exclusive rights to all incoming leads. However, your website needs to have some key components to attract users: a good (mobile and user friendly) design and an implemented SEO strategy to drive traffic to your site.

Websites today need to have a user-friendly interface that is also mobile compatible with a good design scheme to catch the attention of the user. Have you ever been on a site and can't seem to figure out how to navigate through it? You probably didn't stay long on that site before moving on to the next one. You don't want your audience to feel this frustration on your website. So, with a clean and eye-catching design users will navigate through your site seamlessly without the need to go someplace else to find what they are looking for.

Keep in mind that the majority of online visitors maybe searching for their needs on their mobile phones. Your website's design needs to be able to show a consistent representation of your brand for both mobile and desktop users without interfering with the site's design and user friendly aesthetics.

Finally, you need to implement a search engine optimization (SEO) strategy to drive traffic to your site. Unfortunately, this is not something that can happen overnight and won't show progress for some time because search engines need time to build trust with websites. On average, if you are effectively implementing an SEO strategy, you will begin seeing your website rise through the ranks of search engines in 3 to 6 months. Between 6 to 9 months, you will begin to see your website among others on page one of search results, hopefully at the number one position. If you are like many others and don't want to wait, you can use paid ads on search engines like Google AdWords or Bing Ads.

2) Email

Many people seems to believe that email marketing is an outdated lead generating stream; however, it still remains one of the top marketing tactics capable of producing a high return on investment. If done correctly, not only will you see a new flow of potential clients reaching out to you, but you will begin to build trust with them.

An email marketing strategy should build trust with customers and potential leads without overwhelming them with constant emails that will eventually become an annoyance. No one knows your client base better than you, so you would have to figure out the correct number of emails to send on a monthly basis.

When sending emails, personalize emails by adding your client's name to the email's header. Also take into consideration what stage of the buying process your clients are in. For instance, a great way to build trust with a potential lead is by sending them a recent testimonial.

3) Social Media

Through the use of social media, salespersons have a world of leads at their fingertips. Almost everyone you know has a personal account on any number of given networks. This opportunity is yours for the taking and could cost you close to nothing or nothing at all.

When creating your social accounts, create a cohesive look on all your profiles, including your website, to make it easy for followers to recognize your brand. Also, keep in mind that not all social networks are going to benefit you. So before you start creating an account on every social network (and trying to learn how to use it), research your target audience and where they are socializing; see if the platform fills a need another network doesn't, and consider whether or not you have the time to maintain more accounts.

Just like any other form of marketing, you need to implement a social media strategy to help you determine what content you will be posting. Social accounts also need to stay active with a constant flow of content relevant to your business. Every platform differs on how they allow businesses to advertise on their networks. By using paid advertisements on social media you can reach a much greater number of users that you would not otherwise have reached organically. (For a comprehensive look on creating a Facebook Ad, click here.) Finally, whenever creating ads on a social platform, you want to drive the traffic back to your site to fill out a lead generation form.

4) Portals

Portals are a great way to generate leads without emptying your bank account. A large percentage of customers search products on search engines. According to researchers, over 50% of buyers search for their requirements online before ever speaking with a professional.

Whether you prefer traditional or modern methods, utilizing a variety of the techniques mentioned above will give you the best results. Therefore you must focus on creating the best strategy to implement to achieve your desired outcome.

It's easy to move on to the next one after losing a deal and hope for better results next time. However not looking back results in losing out on opportunities to improve.

Chapter 15

Sales Funnel: Creating & Managing IDEA

"Maintaining a healthy sales funnel helps us make accurate forecasts as we can't always just rely on predictions"

Funnel Technique is also called as Sales Funnel Strategy. The sales funnel allows us to envisage leads as they move from total stranger to repeat customer, but it's only a fancy tool if we don't have an effective sales funnel management strategy at workplace.

How to make improvements to your sales funnel over time with data and reporting

What is a sales funnel?

Sales funnel and its importance

A sales funnel is a multi-step process in which prospects become customers.

Visualizing a real-life funnel: the top of the funnel is the widest part where prospects enter through. The bottom of the funnel is a narrow, representing the few of our prospects who will become our customers.

The stages of sales funnels:

The sales funnel is made up of four primary stages:

Stage 1: **Awareness,**

Stage 2: **Interest,**

Stage 3: **Desire,**

Stage 4: Evaluation

Stage 5: Action

(this is the selling "IDEA")

Stage 1: Awareness (top of the funnel)

Prospects: They just got exposure to your product or service.

Company: Generate interest for them to come back when those products or services are required.

Awareness is mostly achieve through marketing efforts which are already discussed in previous chapters.

Stage 2: Interest

Prospects: You've got their attention and they're considering whether or not your product or service would benefit them.

Company: Figure out solutions to their problem. Then demonstrate them how you can help them achieve their goals.

To do this, you'll need to contact your prospects and meet them with their desired information so that you can begin to form a relationship.

When you meet them, take them through various case studies which closely matches with their case. Building rapport with these prospects at this stage will help them trust you through the next stage in the funnel.

Stage 3: Desire

Prospects: They like your products/ services and they want it.

Company: Take them through a clear path to acquire those.

At this stage, the prospect is ready to invest in your product or services. Make doing so as easy as possible for them. Now would be a good time to present positive testimonials and make a mention about guarantees your company upholds. If they're still hesitant, offer them a free trial.

Stage 4: Evaluation

Prospects: They want to evaluate your products or service commitments, perhaps comparatively.

Company: Take this stage seriously and leave no room for prospects to doubt you or your credentials.

The middle of the funnel requires a gentle, nurturing approach. The best way to do this is to continually affirm the prospect that they're making the right choice by purchasing from you.

This is the best time to add testimonials and third-party reviews. People like to see that you can make good on your promise.

The point is, you need to communicate value to your potential customers, whether it's through a guided demo, a free trail or positive word-of-mouth.

Stage 5: Action (bottom of the funnel)

Prospects: They're about to sign the contract and become your customers. These people are ready to commit.

Company: Deliver the customer expectations.

At this stage, the salespersons are about to close the sale. They must thoroughly check the agreement and terms sheet.

Buyer and Seller relationship starts upon closing the sale, send the new customer some useful content to reinforce their confidence in their decision to work with your company. A welcome email with operation & maintenance tips for their new product or service as well as some pointers for realising benefits is a good way to start.

Achieving most from the Selling –"IDEA"

Irrespective of what your sales funnel looks like, a well-managed sales funnel will have the highest concentration of those prospects makes it to the bottom of the funnel.

A good sales funnel management strategy involves

1. a clearly defined sales process:
2. funnel design, based on the sales process,
3. measuring success rate
4. get insights and drive performance.

Invest the time in developing the process, however the initial setup may take some time, depending on how you store your data presently.

Once you've got a solid system is in place, your team can work more efficiently, moving sales through the pipeline with ease—while avoiding the clogs that get in the way.

Focus on relationships.

The most important part of your business is your relationship with your customers. Happy customers become loyal customers and loyal customers are easy to retain.

Business relationship leads to revenue.

In reality customer retention is time and again overlooked even though it's crucial to maximizing your long-term business goals. Make an effort to show your existing customers that you value their continued business.

Various researches have shown that you have a 60 to 70% chance of selling to an existing customer, while you only have about a 5 to 20% chance of selling to a new prospect. Therefore, never ignore them once they've purchased from you.

Finally, collect and review data religiously.

Effective sales funnel technique depend on accessible data. One of the easiest ways to rather and learn from sales data is recording all touch points periodically.

As you spend more time reviewing data, you'll start to identify issues and solutions quickly. Generate weekly funnel reports and form your strategy.

Sales funnel management should provide full order intake visibility and forecast. It's a complete strategy focused on perfecting the finding, qualifying, and closing processes.

Part V

Perform

Chapter 16

Quotes and Follow Up

"Timely submission of the price quotation for product and services is one of the key factor which gets ignored by many salesperson".

How to Prepare a Price Quote

A Product or service proposal document is one of the most important document between customer and the company.

When a customer asks for a price quote, salesperson are often tempted to just give them the total cost of their service or product. But a lot more should go into preparing a good proposal.

Writing a proposal seems to be simple and easy. But the truth is that there's a lot more to think about than just the number because a proposal is a lot more than just the price. It's an opportunity for you to capture the business. It is a window to what the customer can expect if they do business with you. Smart customers can find a lot of information in your quotation well beyond price.

Before the Quote

You receive a call, e-mail or a customer comes to your office asking for a price quotation. Before you prepare the quote, get to know your customer. If you're in the service industry, you'll probably end up at their office but first, qualify them.

Do understand what type of services/ improvements they're looking for? How they address these presently and what is their dissatifcation from present engagement.

Ask yourself, can you handle these services effectively or your product meets their requirement. Can you handover the product/ services within their expected time frame.

Don't waste their time or yours if it's not a job you can do, it's not a product you specialise or if it beyond your area of expertise that you can't get them world-class service.

Next, if you have to visit their place of work or operation, follow some basic rules. Firstly, be on time, keep your words. If you say 10:00 am, be there at 9:55. If another job holds you up, call or text as soon as possible and let them know in advance. Also inform them through a call or text when you're heading to their home. That gives them a reminder to be ready but at the same time also helps to make sure you will find customer who is prepared to discuss.

Look professional. It won't matter to some people but looking clean and neat can be a big deal to some of your prospective customers.

Finally, collect all the information through demo and questions that you need to prepare a precise quote. Get all big and small details. Make your scope of work clear. After you go back work out the price quotation and there shouldn't be any doubts or confusions in your mind.

PLEASE DON'T ASSUME CUSTOMERS' REQUIREMENT

This helps you and indicates your customer that your attention to detail is active. It also helps prevent disagreements over what was thought to be done for the price you proposed.

Perform

As seen in earlier chapters, along the same lines, practice and polish your general sales pitch. Tell your prospective customer about you, your company, what makes you better than your competitors. Also explain them, how you do the work. Customer can relate it more if you can demonstrate your product/ services, maybe with help of some pictures/ videos. Further, offer to give them references.

Inform the customer when you can submit the quote and make sure that you submit the proposal on time. Any delays in submitting the proposal will eventually make the potential customer doubt your commitments. Be professional and remember first impression is last impression.

The Actual Quote

Every business will have different information but in general your quote should have more information than the price. For example, some information about company, some past iconic achievements and some recent accomplishments. Just bullet points or brief summary of thing you presented in your sales pitch. This reinforces customer belief in your products and your company.

While making the quote officially, avoid hand written quotes or one liner emails. The quotation should look professional and official. Every formal or informal communication with the customer communicates a messeage about your company and your professionalism. Further all the communications with the customer must be on record.

The proposal should have your company name, tax numbers, bank details, logo and your contact information.

Itemize the proposal. List all the details or features that you accepted. Your customer wont like to see a number without knowing what it comprises. Set time lines in the proposal itself i.e. completion time and milestone activities.

Consider some room to negotiate. You might quote 5% higher than you normally would in case you have a client that wants to bargain. Along those lines, let them know that if they get a lower quote, you would like a chance to match it.

After the Quote

Once you submit the quote or the proposal, ask them when you should follow up with them. Your customer may wants to see that you're serious about working with them. By and large customer wants attention and therefore they might wait for you to contact them to establish if you're serious. If their requirement is bigger then they would expect involvement of your management too. If they don't give you convenient time to contact them, make a contact in 5 to 7 days.

Always try to find a potential customer or business relationship in the quotation you submit. Don't see a price proposal as just a quote. Utilize this opportunity to take your prospective customer through a model experience they will have with you if they purchase or don't purchase from you. If you see the process just like a transaction, you'll have more customers. It's not merely about price; it's about their total experience.

Chapter 17

Telling isn't Selling

"Just telling about our product or service to our prospective customers while presenting those is the biggest mistake we commit as the salesperson"

Sometimes at the end of sales presentation we hear these word, "I'll think about it...."

If you hear those words too often, then you must introspect and reconsider your sales strategy.

A successful salesperson knows how to guide the prospective customer to "think about it" through sales presentation, thereby completely taking the "I'll think about it" objection off the table. That's also referred to as "the art of mastering a sales presentation."

Before a prospect will purchase a product or service, they need to think about why they need that product or service and how they'll fund it.

One of the biggest mistakes you can make in a sales presentation is simply telling your prospect about your product or service.

Difference between telling and selling

Listing off features, figures and facts about your product or service is not the same as selling it. "Telling isn't selling" ought to be one of your core sales mantras. Without it in mind, you may become a walking, talking pamphlet– a mere information source– rather than an effective salesperson.

Back during my initial days, I learned that I can't simply tell a prospect what my company does. I have to take them through a process that encourages them to think about needing that we did.

By learning to help the prospect think about needing your product or service early on in your sales presentation, you're less likely to hear "I need to think about it" when your presentation comes to a close.

If telling isn't effective, then what is? Asking questions!

Learn to ask the right questions

Each question you ask should serve a purpose. Pose questions that provoke thought, pique interest and make the prospect think about why they need your service now.

In order to answer your questions, prospects have to actively listen and reflect on what you're saying.

Asking a prospect how they feel about something you've said prompts them to consider how they feel now, not later. And remember, emotion can drive sales.

Are you asking closing questions?

It's important to learn to ask "closing questions", questions that lead your prospect to buy into your thinking or your service offering.

For example, if you offer health and wellness coaching, you might ask: "We need an effective wellness programme if we want to reach our health and fitness goals, don't we, John?"

Here, you've asked a question that makes your prospect think about how they have unmet health and fitness goals, and would benefit from investing in the wellness programme you offer so as to stride them closer to achieving those goals.

It also gives them an opportunity to voice any concern they might have, allowing you to address and alleviate that concern.

Likeable salespeople are effective salespeople

It's important to make yourself likeable throughout your presentation. By being genuine, honest and personable, your prospect not only thinks about needing your service but also grows to like and trust you enough to give you their business.

Create comfort with language

One way that you can create rapport is by using warm, caring language, such as saying "we" instead of "you."

Try saying "We deserve better, more sustainable results from our wellness programmes, don't we Alison?"

By positioning yourself as the prospect's friend or a member of their team, you show them that they can relate to you and that you care about their interests.

Let's wrap up with a recap: closing the sale shouldn't begin at the end of your sales presentation.

An effective salesperson asks questions that help the prospect realise why they need your service and demonstrate that it's a great value for the cost.

Many savvy business owners and entrepreneurs understand the sales fundamentals I've laid out but struggle to identify which questions to ask their prospects to help them feel ready to make a purchase decision.

Telling isn't Selling

Closing the sale is an art that takes practice and confidence but it's also a science. Apply a proven formula to your sales presentation consistently and more and more prospects will realise there's nothing left to think about or do, but say "Yes!"

Salespeople often make the mistake of throwing out some product features and benefits, hoping they hit one of the customer's reasons for buying. But people buy for their own reasons and you won't learn what they are unless you listen to them.

"For every action, there is an equal and opposite reaction."

– *Sir Isaac Newton*

A fundamental question in selling is not why people sell but why people buy.

It is well known that people buy for their own reasons–not for the seller's. In fact, their motivation to buy may have very little to do with the reasons why the seller thinks they should buy. When it comes down to it, people buy something to meet their needs or resolve the problems they are facing. According to Neil Rackham, author of SPIN Selling, people decide to buy when "the pain of the problem and desire for a solution have built to the point where they are greater than the cost of the solution."

A good sales professional can help customers come to that realization. But it doesn't happen as easily as you might think. Despite the fact that most people learn the basics of conducting need analysis, customizing solutions and linking benefits to pain in their Sales 101 class but when they are out in the real world they forget to bring these classroom lessons to life and somehow their competence, composure and confidence evaporates. Faced with self-induced, pressure-filled selling situations, they confuse telling with selling.

Equal and Opposite Reaction

As dairy farmers are apt to say, "Cows don't give milk. You have to take it from them." The same is true with selling. Nobody just gives you a sale. You have to take it. But how you "take it" is very counterintuitive. A natural tendency of most sellers is to rush in and as the Newtonian principle outlines, the equal and opposite reaction on part of the buyers is to shut them out.

Like milking a cow, selling can be a delicate operation. While a customer probably won't threaten you with a hoof, you're still faced with the fact that the harder you push, the more push-back you'll get. Why? As President Truman once said: "The best way to give advice to your children is to find out what they want and then advise them to do it." Nobody likes to be told what to do–not even children. Imagine going to a doctor who gives you the same prescription he gave the previous patient because it worked. By not listening, by not being inquisitive, by not clarifying assumptions, sellers come across as not caring–or caring more about themselves–and perpetuate the stereotypes of an arrogant, pushy salesman we all love to hate.

Breathing Your Own Exhaust

So, if you can't tell prospective buyers how good your products and services are for them, how the heck are you supposed to sell? Start by understanding how not to de-sell.

Most salespeople hate dead air. They become anxious. So they make every effort to fill the void by talking incessantly about what they know the most–their own products and services. They get excited about the value they offer and start spewing the features, advantages and benefits.

Unfortunately, the more they talk the more they de-sell and their customers' eyes glaze over and their heels dig in. Customers don't want to be talked at and pushed. They want to be understood. The ancient Greek philosopher Diogenes had it right when he said "We have two ears and one tongue so that we would listen more and talk less." As fundamental as this advice is, not talking can be very difficult for an enthusiastic sales professional.

The greatest conundrum in selling is this: You can't sell without a relationship and you can't have a relationship unless you have sold and demonstrated value. You may be thinking that selling-by-listening only works in one-on-one selling and not in more complex, B2B selling. You would be wrong. No matter how complex the sale, you're still dealing with real people who are making decisions–not faceless corporations. They have the same emotions as anyone else: ambition to do better, fear of failure, confusion with uncertainty, need to be recognized, etc.

Listen and Learn

If telling isn't selling, then what is? What actions can one take to break the vicious cycle and not to generate an undesirable, equal and opposite reaction? Counterintuitive as it sounds, the more successful salespeople are those that ask the most questions. Not just any questions, but smart questions posed in a systematic way. Neil Rackham, in his SPIN Selling Fieldbook, eloquently lays out a systematic approach to asking four types of questions as follows:

Situation: Finding out basic facts about the existing situation and establishing an overall context. This is ideally done through prior research so as not to bore the buyer to tears because they get very little value out of it.

Problem: Asking about the problems, difficulties and challenges the buyer is experiencing with the present situation. People buy only when they have needs and needs almost always start with a dissatisfaction with the status quo. Follow-up questions identify, clarify, and expand the buyer's implicit needs.

Implication: Understanding the consequences and impacts of the situation, thereby transforming implicit needs expressed as problems into explicit needs. They build the significance and seriousness of the problem so that it is large enough to justify action.

Need-Payoff: Checking and assessing the value and usefulness of a solution in a positive and constructive way. They develop the buyer's desire for a solution and move the discussion toward action and commitment.

If you thought that asking questions in this manner is simple, think again. It is enormously difficult to have the confidence and patience to step through these without getting ahead of yourself. It requires tremendous planning, preparation and practice. And most importantly patience.

Patience, My Dear

What makes sellers anxious is the pressure they put on themselves to persuade the buyer. When a sale is seen as a conquest, persuasion naturally becomes the modus operandi and telling appears to be the fastest, easiest and safest way to the victory lap. However, if the sellers adopt a frame of mind to truly understand the buyer's point of view, they are likely to become less anxious. If they seek first to understand, then to be understood, they will be more comfortable in asking questions. Armed with the answers to these questions, they will gain better insights into the buyer's world and will earn the right to help them with a solution.

French philosopher Voltaire was right when he said many centuries ago: "Judge a man by his questions rather than by his answers."

Chapter 18

Handle Objections

Every prospective customer whether first time buyer or existing customer you speak to for new sales will have some objections or reasons that are stopping them from buying your product.

If customer didn't had any reservation about your product or services esp related to price, relevance and their purchasing ability; then they would have already bought it.

A successful salesperson understands how to both discover and resolve these objections.

What is objection handling?

Objection handling is when a prospective customer presents a concern about the product/service a salesperson is selling and the salesperson responds in a way that removes those concerns and allows the deal to move forward. Objections are generally around price, product fit, competitors and after sales service.

Objection handling means responding to the buyer in a way that changes their mind or ease their concerns.

Some aggressive salesperson argue with their prospective customers or try to pressure them into backing down. However this isn't real objection handling. Customers typically end up more convinced than ever of their position and the worse, salesperson

Handle Objections

lose the trust and rapport they've built up.

Instead of telling your customer that they're wrong, help them come to a different conclusion of their own. And if you can't motivate them, that's a sign they're a poor fit.

It's also important to distinguish between sales objections and excuses. While objections are authentic, excuses are lame. Think of an objection as, "We see the value in your product, but We are not sure about buying it for 'XYZ' reason," while an excuse translates to, "We don't want to talk to you." Objections are far more serious than excuses.

An Effective Method for Objection Handling – LEAD.

LEAD involves four steps — Listen Explore Address Discuss

Listen – The Objections;

Explore - The Possible Solution,

Address – Those objection

Decision – Discuss & Decide

When confronted with any objection, firstly listen to the objection carefully and try to figure out its source of origination. This demonstrates to your customer that you are serious about addressing their concern.

The next step is to explore your customer's concern and analyse if there is any impact caused by the concern. You must try to find out the reasons behind the objections. It is important that you investigate and reach the root causes of the objection.

For example, your customer may have stated a price objection but perhaps the real reason they don't want to work with you is because they are loyal to your competition and enjoy the attention provided by them. If you don't take the time to explore with your customer to figure out that they are using "price" as a cover-up objection, then you won't be able to offer appropriate solution.

Hence you must be able to differentiate clearly between an objection and cover-up.

Thirdly, address the objections with facts and figures. Data speaks for itself. As a salesperson you should know the most common objections. You must be ready to address those with facts and references. Your readiness to address customer objections will definitely impress them about your knowledge and you may strengthen your relationship.

The final step is to decide. Only once you have addressed the objection, you can lead the customer to make the decision and close the transaction.

Objection handling is one of the most important and exciting activity for salesperson. It should be viewed as opportunities to help your customer and to develop your relationship with them.

Chapter 19

Sales Negotiation

"In the business as in the life, you don't get what you deserve, you get what you negotiate"

By definition, Negotiation is an act of discussing an issue between two or more parties with the aim of coming to an agreement that addresses the need of everyone involved.

For any salesperson, it is about reaching an agreement like contracts, proposals, commission and compensation plans. However negotiation is a routine activity for every salesperson i.e. for target, commercial terms, schedules, services etc.

Infact a salesperson is negotiating every day. For example, imagine a typical situation you come across at work such as contributing to a task or participating in a meeting.

Let's say you shared your idea with the team. Did they instantly agree with you? Or did you explain your idea in detail and got other team member's input to reach a decision?

That's an example of an everyday negotiation.

During negotiation when the contract value is bigger the stakes may be higher, however you're still going to use the same set of skills to state your case and impact the outcome as you did when you tried to sell your idea to your team.

It is reality, nevertheless, most sellers either avoid negotiations or try to get through them as quickly as possible.

Why is this?

Based on a two-year study of sales negotiations by a research firm, there's good reason to believe this tendency towards avoidance comes from lack of preparation and no formal negotiation process.

The study found:

- Companies with no formal negotiation process had a 63.3% decrease in net income

- Companies with a somewhat formal negotiation process had a 16.2% increase in net income

- Companies with a formal negotiation process experienced a 42.5% increase in net income

80% of the participating companies had no formal negotiation process and 75% of the companies had no negotiation planning tools.

The lack of a formal negotiation plan and process can have major financial ramifications. For example, without a formal sales negotiation process, salespersons often default to discounts in order to close the deal.

This can result in wastage of time and resources when it comes to executing the solution; which also means a lower margin of revenue. This results in lower profit margins.

Even if a salesperson has properly qualified a prospective customer and correctly managed their expectations through the sales process, the deal can still end in a negotiation.

Hence it should be clear now that you need a formal process for sales negotiation.

Skills Required for Sales Negotiation:

The most important negotiation skills in sales are:

Know your limits

"Define the concessions in advance that you're willing to accept".

During negotiation, a 25% discount or additional one year of support might seem perfectly acceptable. It is only when you get back to your laptop and start drafting up the contract that you realize you agreed to terms you shouldn't accept. Clearly defining the limits on price discounts or add-ons before your meeting with the potential customer will ensure you come to a mutually beneficial agreement.

Prospect first

"Let the prospect start the conversation".

You've offered the terms of the deal and the prospective customer would like to negotiate them, so let them go first. In the spirit of being helpful, salespeople are often tempted to offer a rebate before the customer even opens their mouth. But you don't know what they're going to say! It pays to listen first and then speak.

Never give a range.

If the customer would like bargain pricetag of your product then never say, "Well, I could probably reduce the cost by 10 to 15%." Who would accept 10% when 15% has been offered? Always quote one specific number or figure and then go higher or lower if needbe. The word "between" must be avoided at all costs.

Avoid splitting the difference.

According to salesguru, offering to split the difference can do more damage than good. For example, if the product or service costs $10000 and the prospective customer wants it for $5000, the salesperson shouldn't counter with $7500 although it seems logical to do so. If the salesperson offers a small discount but still keeps the number in the neighborhood of the original price, the customer is likely to accept and the margins can be retained.

Avoid putting things in written until the conversation is over.

Negotiations can swing back and forth and all around again. Many thoughts will be proposed and while some will be accepted, others will be rejected. A salesperson would be wise not to revise the proposal document until the meeting has ended and all parties have agreed to the terms.

Negotiate with the decision maker.

This might seem obvious but according to researchers, many salespeople make this mistake of negotiating with the wrong person. This means that you may loose the contract without reaching the right person. This also means that when talks begin with the real decision maker, they will likely start at the already discounted price quoted in the first meeting. A great outcome for the buyer but a poor outcome for the seller.

Get something in return for reductions.

A long-term buyer-seller relationships are built out of mutual respect and trust. With this in mind, salespeople should not accept every single demand of a prospective buyer without making some requests of their own. By keeping the negotiation a win-win for both sides, salesperson and buyer remain on equal footing, which lays the foundation for a mutual beneficial relationship.

Expand the conversation beyond money.

The most commonly negotiated aspect of a sales contract is price, so salesperson should be prepared to talk about pricing. However, since price is linked to value and value is linked to a customer's perception of and satisfaction with a product. Therefore, salesperson should consider offering other add-ons in lieu of a reduced price tag. However, keep in mind that the specific concessions a salesperson can offer depends on the situation.

Keep the conversation light and graceful.

Although buyer and salesperson sit on opposite sides of the table during a negotiation, they will be partners if the deal is signed. Keep the talk smooth and jovial to avoid creating bad experience.

Walk away if necessary.

Salespeople should understand and clearly distinguish between reasonable and unreasonable demands. If the demands become unreasonable or unprofitable for the company, be brave to walk away from the deal. A customer who only agreed to sign if the contract was drastically amended or the price was radically dropped is bound to cause problems down the road. Further, they clearly don't see much value in the offering, it's only a matter of time before they become dissatisfied. Hence please walk out for your own and your customer's sake.

The salesperson often needs to shift gears from salesman to consultant to negotiator in order to bring about an agreement that is a win-win for both companies. While negotiations can go in a seemingly infinite number of directions, salesperson with the above negotiation skills will be better equipped to roll with the punches.

Part VI

Post-Sales

Chapter 20

Customer Support and Service

An organisation is judged by their after customer service and sales support. It includes activities like contract fulfilment, billing, collection, alterations, cancellation, returns, complaints and service support.

Contract fulfilment includes arranging the product/ services as specified within agreed time frame. Therefore any over commitment made during signing the contract will be reflected here.

Billing includes customer details billing address, shipping address, tax numbers, contact person details and information. Even a small mistake in the bill can cost a lot. Hence, when stakes are high check the billing information and ask customer for confirmation.

Collection means collecting the payment as per contract/ company policy. It includes advance, cash against product and outstanding if any. Outstanding can be real challenge for survival of an organisations.

Alterations, change in product/ services specification:- Some changes are easy to manage. However some changes are not possible or has a greater impact on cost. Negotiate alterations carefully.

Customer Support and Service

Returns/ Complaints: There is a possibility that customer is not satisfied with the product as it might not have fulfilled customer's expectation. In such cases, act as per contract.

Cancellation: There can be situation when customer cancels the contract or job due to their internal issues or due to delay in supplies. A reputed company must deal with the cancellation with care. Losing a customer can't an acceptable solution for any company or organisation.

Training/ Product Support

You should have a system in place i.e. product support system.

The main aim of this system is to provide product support to help your customer understand your product so that they know how to use your product; such that they maximize the value of the product.

Here are some indicators for providing product support.

Create a resource page on your website specifically for your product. Depending on your product and based on your customer feedback create a Do/ Not To Do list. Also create FAQ list with clear answers.

Instruction manual

Having an Instruction manual in form of a specific page to provide to customers will save you time from answering simple queries. The time you save can be put to answering more complex or technical queries. Uploading a youtube video can help customers a lot.

Focus on advantages while creating content related to product support. The reasons why they bought the product are likely based on the paybacks you stressed to your customers, so these are the benefits and features that you need to focus on explaining carefully to your customers.

Have a transparent, brief replace and refund policy for faulty or damaged products. Be clear on the terms, requirements, and what your customers need to know or do for return of the damaged products and get a refund. Ensure that your policy uses clear, upfront language and that the policy favours your customer so that it doesn't make it hard for customers to follow the policy.

Uphold money-back guarantees: Money-back guarantees are predominantly useful for digital products or services. In case returns aren't really applicable yet there's a chance that customer can be dissatisfied with your product for whatever reason, in such case refund the money.

Get back to product support inquiries as soon as you possibly can. When your customer sends a product support inquiry, every minute it's unresolved is one minute that they're less than satisfied with your product. Address concerns and problems as soon as you can preferably within 12 hours if possible.

If you find yourself scrambling frantically to answer all these inquiries, you might need to look into hiring some freelancers or even a full-time employee to help you reply to these inquiries quickly.

Customer Service

Customer service involves taking care of your customers' needs by providing and delivering valuable service and assistance before, during, and after the customers' requirements are met.

Customer service covers your entire sales process, from pre-sales to closing to post-sales and so much so that even product support counts towards customer service.

Customer Support and Service

But customer service is most significant during the post-sales process because once your customers have received their products, the quality of your customer service is then a huge deciding factor of whether your customer will be a repeat customer or not. Also, happy customers will give you honest and constructive feedback on multiple aspects of your business.

Satisfied customers become loyal advocates and make for great advertising.

Communicate clearly and plainly. No one likes getting the runaround. When having conversations with your customers, go straight to the point and use language that's easy to understand.

Don't be afraid to ask questions. There will be times that your customers' concerns won't be obvious at the onset or on their initial contact. It's now your job to dig deeper and ask probing questions.

Remain professional and polite whatever happens. No matter how agitated or combative your customers are, never lose your cool. Remain professional in your tone and your word choice. Being polite without being condescending goes a long way toward defusing a potentially tense conversation.

Be positive. Using positive language doesn't mean you should act cheerful when your customers are having issues; it means using phrases that are constructive, inspire positive action and comforting to the customer.

Positive phrasing tells what could be done instead of what can't be done, suggests alternatives instead of placing blame, and emphasizes positive actions and rewards that they can anticipate getting instead of pointing out the negative consequences.

For example, starting a sentence with "You claim that…" implies

Post-Sales

that they're lying, while starting a sentence with "As I understand it..." implies that you read what they're saying and you're attempting to comprehend them.

Be honest. Part of being straightforward and transparent is being absolutely truthful in all your communications. Never promise anything you can't deliver and always follow through on your word.

Don't let them go until you've solved your customers' concern. From your perspective, all these customers are asking the same questions and having the same issues. But for your customers, their issues are individually important to them. Treat these issues as such and make it a habit to confirm with your customers whether you've resolved their issues to their satisfaction.

This information allows you to see if there are any issues that the majority of your customers are experiencing so you can do something about it. Having meticulous records also allows you to review how you communicate with your customers and look for footprints of improvement.

These logs also serve as proof in case you ever get a feedback that you never got back to a customer when you actually did or when customers allege that you promised something when you never did.

Use the right tools. If you're in this by yourself, you might not want to have customers call you; not because you're not committed to customer service but simply because it's not practical for your business.

Social media is actually a great venue for customer service but only if you actually engage with them. Live chat is also a good venue for customer service but again, only if you set proper expectations for the turnaround time.

You can also set up a discussion forum area on your website to crowdsource answers to common questions and concerns about your product, which can also serve as a resource page for your new and potential customers.

Finally, email support is also a good tool for customer service, as probably everyone who orders products online would have an email address and would use emails to communicate.

Chapter 21

Relationship Management

A post-sales process is a number of tasks that you perform after your customer buys a product from you. Once your customer receives the product from you, that's when your post-sales process kicks in.

Many of salesperson think that process is over and they need to move to next call. Moving to next call is important, however taking existing customer along is equally important. They are the ones who show you the mirror.

1. It strengthens your relationship with your customers.

Perhaps the most important purpose of an effective post-sales process is that it ensures that your customers are satisfied with your product and their overall buying experience.

Providing excellent product support and customer service guarantees that your customers make the most out of the product they bought from you.

2. It builds your reputation.

When you meet your customers' needs and solve their pain points sufficiently, that enhances their opinion for you and results in a positive word of mouth. Recommendations from existing customers can actually be more influential than other types of promotion, such as through social media or through advertising.

3. It improves your product.

This may be an indirect result, but getting plenty of useful feedback is a great way to know what you need to keep and what you need to improve in terms of your actual product.

4. It compels you to evaluate your target audience, product, and entire sales process.

In order to enhance customer experience, many organisations have started using Customer Relationship Management – CRM Software.

Below figure explains CRM integration.

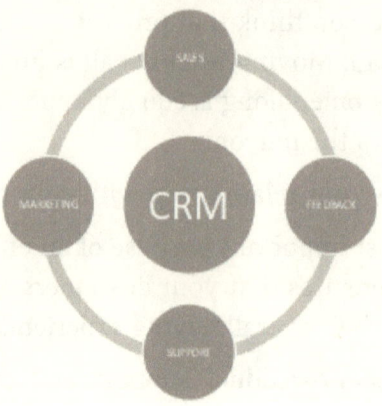

CRM Software is a software tool that's designed to help customers of the organisation a unique and seamless experience as well as build better relationships by providing a complete picture of all customer interactions, keeping track of sales, organising and prioritising opportunities. It also facilitate collaboration between various teams.

When you've been selling for a while, you get comfortable with

Post-Sales

your process and you might think that as long as your entire process is working, there's no need to take a look at it again.

But business environment is fast-changing and a process that works today may not be working tomorrow. Continual evaluation of all your processes enables you to survive.

Chapter 22

Customer Feedback & Evaluation

Getting customer feedback helps you know your customers better. It also enables you to incorporate necessary changes in your product, process and customer service for greater customer satisfaction.

Customer feedback is essential because while customer-initiated comments and assessments are very useful, you can't rely solely on them. It is said that for every customer who bothers to complain, 10 other customers remain silent. These silently dissatisfied customers likely wouldn't come back to you for business and you won't see them again.

Following are some ways to gather customer feedback:

- Welcome kit/ Welcome message after purchase confirmation.

- Dedicated email address, phone number and contact for customer support.

- Link customer email address or contact form to newsletters and other regular correspondences

- Community monitoring: Observe self-hosted forum on website

- Social listening: Monitor social media posts and comments as well as posts on other forums

- Market research survey through email, social media and newsletters

- Phone Call/ Email survey when order is lost.

Consider feedback as a tool to open a dialogue. Receiving and accepting feedback shouldn't be the end of your communication with your customers; instead, consider it as the start of a constructive interaction.

Ask the precise questions. If you want sincere answers, you'll have to ask right questions. Here are some examples to get you started.

Keep it simple and easy to answer your questions. Answering surveys is optional, customers can always choose not to do it. Simplify your questions and use as few questions as you probably can.

The best of all is a customer satisfaction survey that also includes an open-ended question which allows customers to express freely.

Offer incentives/ rewards:- Answering feedback can be an inconvenience; a slight one but an inconvenience nonetheless. If you can provide some kind of gift or freebie, your customers might be more inclined to answer the questionnaire, especially the longer ones.

Use the customer feedback you receive wisely. Positive and negative feedback are both extremely useful for your business.

Positive feedback: The positive feedback can be used as a benchmark of what you're doing right. Also you can use positive feedback as a social proof of your product with the respondents' permission.

Negative feedback: Negative feedback is like an alarm to pull up your socks. These can actually be more useful. Unflattering comments about your products or anything else about the customer experience let you identify points of improvement.

In addition, negative comments or posts given publicly such as on social media or public forums are opportunities to display professionalism. Apologize, respond to their feedback, rectify the situation and end on a hopeful note that you've resolved their issue.

Evaluation

Surveys have some advantages since they ask explicit questions which can be analysed and trended over time. This allows you to measure the extent to which business strategy or policy changes have impacted customer satisfaction.

It is an important task to analyze customer feedback that arrive in as a comment or answer to open-ended question.

Evaluating each answer or remark will be helpful in understanding the needs of individual customers. However, you'll gain more information if you review the comments in batches and attempt to uncover patterns in the answers by categorizing them.

Once you've gone through the comments, you will notice that the comments fall into categories. For example sample categories could include factors such as time, speed, accuracy, courtesy, price, availability, hours, location, etc. depending upon the product and services.

Once you have identified categories according to your business, review the comments again. This time you will be able to group comments into appropriate category.

You will also notice that some comments are positive and some are negative. It's possible to have both positive and negative comments in some categories. Therefore, you may need to divide categories into 2 parts i.e. area of improvement for negative comments and area of excellence for positive comments.

After all of the comments are categorized, look for patterns. During your customer analysis, the patterns will usually correlate to the themes you're seeing in the quantitative portion of your questionnaire. Your customer satisfaction survey analysis will add substantial value to your quantitative research by providing customer insight into what went wrong and what would make it right.

Hence a careful analysis of customer feedback and taking action based on customer comments can help you turn the knob and open a new gate for your team's success.

Periodically take time to look at your post-sales data and analyze them. Assess your product and services. Are your customers satisfied? Would they recommend your product and services to others?

Assess your entire sales process. Were your market research and product research perfect? Were your marketing efforts effective? Did you attract the right audience for your product?

Assess your target customers. Are your customers happy with your website, product and your communications with them? Are you still meeting their needs? Finally, are you still targeting the right audience?

An effective post-sales process allows you to support your

Customer Feedback & Evaluation

customers to get the most out of your product, foster customer loyalty and get feedback to help you improve your business. All of these go a long way toward customer retention.

In business you want more customers because that increases sales leading to increase in your profit. Since it's harder and costlier to acquire new customers than keeping existing ones, customer retention must be one of your key goals and top priority.

www.ingramcontent.com/pod-product-compliance
Lightning Source LLC
Chambersburg PA
CBHW020917180526
45163CB00007B/2768